WHAT PEOPLE ARE SAYING ABOUT
THE GOD-WILD MARRIAGE

"The most valuable and enlightening books originate from a journey. As someone who knows, appreciates, and respects Steve Holt, I can tell you that he's the real deal. So is his marriage. These pages are far more than the result of some computer keys being tapped, they are the outcome of a marriage being lived out in real ways—unpacking the wisdom of God fleshed out in an authentic couple's journey. The refreshing insights are both biblical and practical, and thousands of couples have been impacted by them. Whether your marriage is on the rise or on the rocks, the ready-to-apply wisdom in these pages is well worth your time and energy."

Matt Heard
Senior Pastor
Woodmen Valley Chapel

"Steve Holt begins his premise on a wild marriage with the only foundation that will survive: on God. So many marriages include God but are not built on God, with God and for God's glory. I love that the applications of this book flow directly out of a Christocentric interpretation of God's book. I highly recommend this book. It will help many marriages."

Scott Thomas
Acts 29 Network

"This book is biblically sound, practically relevant, and Spirit-empowered. And the author lives the message. I know. I'm his brother and have spent significant time in his home! I promise he didn't pay me to say all of this."

Dr. David Holt
Pastor and author
Pastoring with Passion

"Whether we realize it or not, what all of us long for is a marriage worthy of being called God-scripted—where Christ and His character is at the very center of our union. Our friend Pastor Steve Holt has written a powerful book that will transform your view on marriage, laying down your life for your spouse, and fulfilling your God-given mission as a couple. You will be encouraged and blessed to be God's best for your spouse!"

Kay and Julie Hiramine
Founders
Generations of Virtue Ministry

"I am so grateful my friend Steve Holt has written this book. Every marriage is under attack, and we all need encouragement and sound teaching to survive and then thrive with our spouses. I believe this book will help all of us in our journey."

Brady Boyd
New Life Church
Author of Sons and Daughters

"Pastor Steve and Liz have had a God-wild marriage now for 26 years. He has loved well and wildly his beloved Liz. In the pages of *God-Wild Marriage,* you will have the opportunity to learn from his and Liz's experiences with Scripture as the backdrop to gather yourself and your spouse for the great adventure of loving one another wildly for a lifetime. Don't just have a marriage, let Steve show you how to have a God-wild marriage!"

Kelly Williams
Author
Real Marriage

"Steve Holt's biblical and candid look at the adventure of a Jesus-centered marriage will create a passion in you to get out of control. His story offers real-life help to empower and encourage you in your most important commitment. You will be inspired to experience your own adventure as you read this."

Daniel Rolfe
Lead Pastor
Mountain Springs Church

"Look around at the married couples in our churches and community and it's clear that something's missing. Too many marriages are failing. Even the intact ones look fatigued. If the missing element in marriage is vision (and I believe it is), then Steve Holt's *God-Wild Marriage* provides some welcomed lenses. By walking through Ephesians 5 in a practical, biblical, relevant and humble way, Steve encouraged me to see my own marriage through the lens of a higher calling. *God-Wild Marriage* roots daily marriage in a vision to pursue our spiritual calling in the power of the Holy Spirit. It blends important how-to's of marriage to the oft-missing how-comes. The result is a renewed and compelling vision for the process God uses to make two people into one."

Mark Schatzman
Teaching Pastor, Fellowship Bible Church of Northwest AR
Speaker with FamilyLife's Weekend to Remember marriage conference

THE GOD-WILD MARRIAGE

A ROADMAP TO A DANGEROUSLY FULFILLING LOVE LIFE

S T E V E   H O L T

PUBLISHED BY ALLIANCE PUBLISHING GROUP, INC.

COPYRIGHT INFORMATION

THE GOD-WILD MARRIAGE
A Roadmap to a Dangerously Fulfilling Love Life
© 2012 Steve Holt

Published by Alliance Publishing Group, Inc.
P.O. Box 190405
Birmingham, Alabama 35219

Unless otherwise noted, all Scripture quotations are taken from the New King James Version.® Copyright ©1982 by Thomas Nelson, Inc. Used by permission. All rights reserved.

First Printing, 2012

ISBN: 978-0-9836814-1-0

Printed in the United States of America

Cover Design by Anna Holt
Interior Design by Vic Wheeler

DEDICATION

TO LIZ
Relish life with the spouse you love
*Ecclesiastes 9:9 (*The Message*)*

TO JOE AND MELBA
A beautiful heritage
Jeremiah 3:19

ACKNOWLEDGEMENTS

The two greatest events of my life were being chosen by Jesus to be His follower and being chosen by Liz to be her husband. Without either, this book could not be written. It's all grace. The constant love, power, and forgiveness of both have transformed my life. Truly, I have lived a God-wild adventure in relationship to Jesus and Liz. Thank you Jesus. Thank you Liz.

My parents, Joe and Melba, provided the context for meeting Jesus and Liz. My dad, as a church planter and pastor, always passionately loved Jesus and mom, in that order. Dad's spiritual leadership and mom's gracious way in following dad's leadership laid foundations that set my values in being a husband and father. The older I get, the more I realize how important this early home life was in building the present life I'm now living. Thank you mom and dad.

My children, Anna, Daniel, Deborah, Isaac, Samuel, Joshua, and Charity, are the canvas on which Liz and I have painted our lives. Their constant support and joy have made our home my absolute favorite place to be each day. Thanks guys.

I'd also like to thank Karla Dial Schneeberger for her editorial changes, tweaks, and inspired ideas. She is the one who most helped this first-time writer stay focused, find precise wording, and move toward well-structured writing. Thank you Karla.

I'd like to thank Marc Fey for his encouragement to write the book, showing me that it could be done, especially at a time when I wanted to quit. Marc, do you remember all our conversations at our sons' baseball games?

Finally, I want to thank Paul Stanley, Jerry Wilson, David Holt, Peter and Peggy Marsh, and many others who read chapters of the book and gave encouragement and helpful comments that added so much to its content. I can't thank all of you individually, but I'm deeply grateful.

TABLE OF CONTENTS

THE POWER OF THE HOLY SPIRIT

[18] And do not be drunk with wine, in which is dissipation; but be filled with the Spirit, [19] speaking to one another in psalms and hymns and spiritual songs, singing and making melody in your heart to the Lord, [20] giving thanks always for all things to God the Father in the name of our Lord Jesus Christ, [21] submitting to one another in the fear of God.[a]

MARRIAGE — CHRIST AND THE CHURCH

[22] Wives, submit to your own husbands, as to the Lord. [23] For the husband is head of the wife, as also Christ is head of the church; and He is the Savior of the body. [24] Therefore, just as the church is subject to Christ, so let the wives be to their own husbands in everything.

[25] Husbands, love your wives, just as Christ also loved the church and gave Himself for her,[26] that He might sanctify and cleanse her with the washing of water by the word, [27] that He might present her to Himself a glorious church, not having spot or wrinkle or any such thing, but that she should be holy and without blemish. [28] So husbands ought to love their own wives as their own bodies; he who loves his wife loves himself. [29] For no one ever hated his own flesh, but nourishes and cherishes it, just as the Lord does the church. [30] For we are members of His body,[b] of His flesh and of His bones. [31] "For this reason a man shall leave his father and mother and be joined to his wife, and the two shall become one flesh."[c][32] This is a great mystery, but I speak concerning Christ and the church. [33] Nevertheless let each one of you in particular so love his own wife as himself, and let the wife see that she respects *her* husband.

Ephesians 5:18-33
New King James Version

FOREWARD

L et me begin these next few paragraphs by saying that Beverley, my wife, and I have been married for 54 years. It seems that in "marriage lingo" that is a very long time. In reality, it is. During those five decades we have had many ups and downs, but we have had a resolve that the marriage vow was something to be taken very seriously. The words we exchanged those many years ago in a little church in Denair, California, were filled with promises to one another, but even more importantly, to God Himself. The fact that He ordained the ceremony and created the institution makes it more than just a fancy event filled with stress and festivity. "'Til death us do part" is a not a phrase to be taken casually, but one that is to be spoken with reverence and mutual intent.

Over my half century in ministry—both as a pastor and Vice President at Focus on the Family—I married hundreds of couples. I do not have a good read on how many of those marriages have been successful or gone the distance, but I am pretty sure that my "batting average" has not been much better than the national statistics indicate. That is very disappointing because most of these couples had a church connection or at least, through pre-marriage counseling, an overview of what to expect. Reality took its toll on their relationships, and what was intended to be a life-long journey together ended sadly and painfully.

Steve Holt and his wife Liz have been my friends for several years. Bev and I have been with them socially, and I have had the privilege of serving as a mentor to Steve. Our conversation has been varied and far reaching. We have talked about just about everything related to the church, pastoral families and the onslaught Satan has waged against those in our churches. Specifically, we have addressed the subject of failed marriages. So intrigued was Steve with this challenge that for the past five years, he has been attempting to address the subject in a very practical and biblical method. And now in this book—*The God-Wild Marriage*—he has captured the essence of what the Apostle Paul was saying in Ephesians chapter five. It is not your typical "five steps to a happy marriage," or an exercise in communication. His very first chapter makes the point that "marriage does not begin with your spouse, it begins with God." This is not a startling statement, but it is one that is so often overlooked. Really!

Sure, you will examine the subjects of communication, intimacy, submission, Christ-like love, and selflessness, but it will be presented to you in a novel, energetic, practical, and applicable manner that can be "caught"—applied to your own marriage and "taught"—as a teachable tool to help others succeed in their marriages. In time *The God-Wild Marriage* will become a classic, but for now it is an anointed look at what God intended His Institution—marriage—to be.

I look back at the beginning days of my marriage. I had so little preparation for what was ahead and very few resources to help me navigate the hazards. I did not have *The God-Wild Marriage* that puts the challenges all of us face in such vivid perspective. Now I do; and so do you.

My prayer is that God will use the thoughts and words He has given Steve Holt both to prepare those who are anticipating a Holy Union, and those of us who are looking to enrich our relationships—a responsibility that will never go away, even after 54 years.

H.B. London,
Pastor to Pastor Emeritus, Focus on the Family;
President of H.B. London Ministries

INTRODUCTION

By all means marry. If you get a good wife, you'll become happy.
If you get a bad one, you'll become a philosopher.

Socrates

A magnificent marriage begins not with knowing one another
but with knowing God.

Gary and Betsy Ricucci

There must be a story behind that quote by Socrates. He was, after all, a philosopher. Socrates must have understood something that I have known for years—marriage is dangerous.

When I was an all-around gymnast at the University of Georgia, one of the events I liked the most was the high bar. The high bar routine is a combination of exhilaration and fear, involving twists, turns, and releases some ten to fifteen feet above the gym floor. Marriage is like that too: It's one of the most adventurous and fulfilling relationships you will ever know and yet fraught with risk and danger.

Some of the maneuvers performed on the high bar involve the gymnast releasing the bar and, for a time, hanging in midair. Most high bar crashes happen during catch-and-release moves, making that midair moment a split-second and thrilling time of danger, anticipation, and uncertainty. It's absolutely wild.

Paul Tournier, in his book, *A Place for You*, describes such an in-between experience—between the time we leave home and arrive at our destination; between the time we leave childhood and arrive at adulthood; between the time we leave doubt and arrive at faith.[1]

Similarly, the book you are holding is a kind of roadmap to a wild and dangerous adventure helping you successfully navigate the journey of marriage. It may require you to willingly release the conventional bar of what you thought marriage is while you float in midair for a while, looking at marriage as it was truly meant to be. We will look at one of the most powerful biblical high bars on marriage ever written—Ephesians 5:18-33. As you read, your cultural concepts of relationships, and especially the marriage relationship, may be challenged, requiring you to let go of the old ways in order to catch a new way of thinking, and subsequently, a new way of living.

Know this: It's the in-between time, the hanging in midair, that will be the most uncomfortable, full of moments of floating and anticipation—of learning new ways of thinking and new ways of relating—that will fill you with either faith or fear. I want to challenge you to embrace the fear, ask God for faith, and watch Him remold and remodel your marriage into a God-wild adventure.

I once had a counseling session with a married couple who were close friends of ours. He was a successful lawyer, and his wife was a lovely person who enjoyed being a mother to their four children. On the outside, everything seemed ideal—and even as we talked and they both shared their frustrations with the other person, no concrete problems seemed to exist. On further investigation, however, it became apparent that they had lost their passion for each other. A kind of boredom had set in.

Boredom—we might even call it tameness—is a dangerous threat to most marriages. If your marriage is like most couples', somewhere along the way, the fun, romance, expectation, and anticipation of a better life has gotten lost in the complexities of day-to-day living; differences in personality and the pressures of jobs, finances, and children have worn you down. Routine has set in, and the wild adventure you had hoped for has become boring, about as exciting as watching a rerun of *Seinfeld*. You have a tame marriage.

One recent report about how young people are choosing to wait longer before getting married now than in the past revealed that the most frequent reason for delaying marriage is the lack of joy they saw in their parents' relationships—and their subsequent divorces.[2]

But God designed marriage to be a wild, adventurous following of Jesus! Jesus is not tame, and you and your spouse—as God has made you to be—are not tame either. The reason I know this is that Liz and I have not had a conventional marriage. In almost everything, we are as opposite as the north is from the south. We have had some terrific fights! But we have also stayed committed to the adventure of following Jesus together. Through job changes, international relocations, many failures, and raising seven children, we have fought for the adventure of marriage. And, now in our fifties, after all the battles, we are grateful. As we too see so many of our friends hitting the midlife years and quitting their boring marriages, we know their situations could be so much better. We also have many friends whose marriages are wild, still adventurous, and full of anticipation for what lies ahead.

This book is all about how to recapture, or to capture for the first time, God's best for your marriage. It's also an invitation to discover new treasure in Ephesians 5:18-33, leading to a God-wild, adventurous marriage! At the end of the day, you will know yourself better—as He has designed you to be. You'll know your spouse better, and most valuable of all, you will know Jesus better—the author and designer of your faith-filled, God-wild marriage.

MARRIAGE FOR DUMMIES

I met Liz in China. We had our first date in Hong Kong, fell in love in Los Angeles, and got married in Tokyo. Our first two children were literally "made in Japan." Today, we've been married for more than 20 years, have lived on two continents, and are raising seven children. Now, most of you have not lived in another culture and are certainly not choosing to have enough children to make up a basketball team (with substitutes on the bench). The choices we have made, along with the complexities of trying to keep a marriage and home together, have made the journey intense at times. This book is an outgrowth of our journey with each other and with God. It's an autobiographical, biblical, and spiritual search for the deep desires of our hearts—a purposeful, fulfilling, passionate, wildly fruitful marriage. Through the process, we've discovered a wildly loving God who has given us a marriage manual that works.

I just read on Facebook this week that marriage is "on its way out, like the dinosaurs." Irrelevant. Extraneous. Inconsequential. That's what many people, particularly this generation, have concluded about marriage. Could it be that people in the Twenty-First Century have learned, through the example of many failed marriages, that it just doesn't work in the modern world? That it was an idea for a slower, simpler time?

It could be. But I have good news! God has written the ultimate "Marriage for Dummies" manual—the Bible—clearly enough for even the simplest of us to understand. Because this Book tells the story of His love for His followers, it illustrates for us how to love in the most challenging and rewarding situation of all, marriage. In fact, throughout the Bible, God metaphorically uses marriage as the *main symbol* for His covenant relationship with His people.[3] God paints the picture of His love for us as that of a lovesick lover in the Old Testament and as a bridegroom in the New Testament.[4]

I'm a pastor, and my main style of teaching is taking our congregation through the Bible chapter by chapter and verse by verse—what we call C by C and V by V. It was on such a journey through the book of Ephesians that God opened up my eyes to His plan for marriage and family.

Though I was preparing a series of messages for the congregation, God met me in a very personal way, one that impacted my own marriage profoundly. It was while studying late one night that my eyes were opened to new possibilities. As I dug into the book of Ephesians, I was awe-struck by God's wildly adventurous, yet ordered design for the marriage relationship—one that includes the power of God, the role of Jesus, and the unique roles of the man and the woman.

I discovered that Chapter 5 of Ephesians captures the heart of God for the marriage relationship. One commentator writes, "The longest statement in the New Testament on the relationship of husbands and wives is Ephesians 5:21-33."[5] The grand theme of Ephesians is the dual focus on Christ and His relationship with the church—the mystery of God's love for the church.[6] In his exhortation to husbands, Paul builds his argument for intimacy in marriage through his design for intimacy between Christ and the church: "Husbands, love your wives, just as Christ also loved the church." Speaking of this same verse, John Piper writes, "Marriage refers to Christ and the church—every marriage … even if the couple doesn't care about Jesus."[7] W.J. Larkin sums this up adeptly when he comments, "the instruction for conduct in marriage in Ephesians 5:22-33 becomes unquestionably binding when seen as a reflection of Christ's relation to the church."[8] Paul is giving us a clear glimpse into the God-centered, Spirit-empowered, passionate, God-wild marriage.

A GOD-WILD EXCURSION

We will delve into a verse-by-verse exploration of what God says about experiencing this wild marriage. Each verse builds on the last. God has a divine order not only for marriage, but for home life, too. We've entitled this book *The God-Wild Marriage* because most, if not all, of God's principles and exhortations found here are wild! The gospel of Jesus was at the time of its writing, and remains today, the wildest good news ever proclaimed. It's wildly different from what our culture tells us; it is wildly extravagant in its implications. The principled points of each verse are counterintuitive and countercultural,[9] and quite frankly are not heard much in Christian counseling today. Much of what God is teaching here is not popular and may even make you mad. As a result, this may be the most challenging book you will read this year.

Since I began teaching this material, thousands of couples have been impacted. So get ready for an adventure. God's design for marriage in Ephesians 5:18-33 may open your heart and bring a new freedom and purpose to your life.

I'm saddened by how many of us, even those of us who call ourselves Christians, are missing the key elements of a meaningful marriage. As a pastor, I regularly counsel couples who are clueless about the design and purpose for their marriage. So I have set up this discussion about marriage to follow it just as the Lord taught it to me—a study through Ephesians 5. This book will open your mind and heart to a God who loves you and has provided His sovereign power for you and your spouse as you discover His design for your marriage.

Let me emphasize this: God is wildly excited about marriage—and especially *your* marriage. He has created you, your spouse, and the marriage relationship to be the main vehicle for you to experience His extravagant love, forgiveness, and power. God wants your marriage to be the place where His power and holiness are most evident. If we follow His design, it will be an experience like no other.

It is my prayer that you, too, will be able to uncover the wonderful treasure of God's Word. I pray that you will hear God Himself reveal through the pages of this book a wonderful vision for your marriage. It is a new day indeed for you and your spouse.

I invite you to a high bar routine. Likely, it will be both exciting and frightening. As a result of what you read, God will call you to release the old bar of a tame relationship and re-catch the new bar of a wild God. Enter at your own risk. Grab the bar.

CHAPTER 1:
THE POWER TO BE OUT OF CONTROL

A journey is like a marriage. The certain way to be wrong is to think you can control it.
John Steinbeck

Only God can satisfy the hungry heart of man.
Hugh Black

And do not be drunk with wine, in which is dissipation; but be filled with the Spirit ...
Ephesians 5:18

I like being in control. As an athlete, I captained most of the teams I played on. As a senior in high school, I was the student body president and enjoyed telling the principal how to run the high school. (You think I'm kidding? I'm not.) Then I got married.

Marriage changed everything.

Liz doesn't like to be controlled. It took me about one day into our honeymoon to realize that I had signed up for a role that was frighteningly different than any other. We were in Hawaii, and I wanted to get up early on the first day, hit the beach, go snorkeling, and then dive off some nearby cliffs ... before breakfast. I thought it was all so ordinary. Wouldn't anyone want to begin a honeymoon in such a way? Fat chance.

My wife wasn't going to be controlled.

Liz was exhausted. The wedding ceremony less than 36 hours

earlier and a torrential rainstorm and flood just before we left Tokyo, coupled with an eight-hour flight to Hawaii, was enough to keep her in bed for at least one day. I couldn't relate.

For me, it was a case of, "You only come to Hawaii once, let's get rolling." It was time for fun on the beach, adventure, and action! But for Liz, it was a time to recover and relax—her way. A heated argument inaugurated our first day of marriage. I lost, she won. So much for my ways; so much for my control.

All of us want to be in control of our lives. All of us want our way—because it's the right way, right? All of us are enslaved to a need for control that has infused and impacted our thinking, making it virtually impossible to understand God's design for a wildly fruitful marriage. This was no less true in biblical times than it is today. When Paul wrote to the Ephesians, he would have been aware of the well-known cultural axiom: "Every Roman man must have a concubine for pleasure, a mistress for adventure, and a wife for progeny." Western culture is no different.

For all of our focus on control, however, marriages today are indeed out of control. The typical couple walking down the aisle is guaranteed a marriage that will last about seven years, a span of time that is shorter than the life of their washer, dryer, or refrigerator. As unbelievable as it may seem, the divorce rate in America has increased by over 200 percent in just the last forty years.[10] The Pew survey on marriage, the largest ever conducted, found that nearly 40 percent of us think marriage is obsolete.[11] (It is interesting that of those who said marriage is headed for extinction, only 5 percent said they don't want to be married.[12] Hmmm.) If you're the product of a broken home, your chances for a tumultuous, difficult marriage are even greater.[13]

As one who regularly counsels couples, I can tell you the family in general and marriage in particular is in real trouble. Couples are ditching their commitment to marriage at an alarming rate, even those who attend church—*especially* alarming for those who attend church.

According to the Barna Group, those who call themselves "born-again" Christians have a higher rate of divorce than non-believers (27 percent compared to 23 percent). Those who label themselves "fundamentalist" Christians have the highest divorce rate of all, at 30 percent.

I once asked my mom if she had ever thought about divorcing my dad. "No, I've never considered divorce," she replied, "but murder? Yes." She was being humorous, but the struggle was real and *is* real. In just this past year, Liz and I have been continually shocked to watch many of our close friends filing for divorce. Many a morning, we have sat across from each other in our breakfast nook and wept over and prayed about dear friends who are leaving their marriages. Discussing with these couples how and why they have decided to break up has been heartwrenching.

Every marriage is hard. Every marriage is a battleground. You may be feeling this way right now. Your marriage has not turned out to be what you had hoped and dreamed. The "storybook" romance you thought you were signing up for has actually turned into some kind of Shakespearean tragedy. Your Prince Charming has turned into a frog. Your relationship with your spouse is an endless foray into verbal arguments, quiet distance, or both. You probably have felt at times like you have a marriage lost in space—your husband is from Mars; your wife is from Venus.[14]

OUT OF CONTROL

Have you come to the realization that you can't control your spouse? Have you been married long enough to realize that two people from entirely different backgrounds, with different values and different views on so many things, aren't going to change each other very much? After twenty-five years of marriage, Liz and I have changed very little in our basic worldviews, personalities, and perspectives. Has it dawned on you that you don't have the power to have a happy marriage?

If so, you just might be in a better place than you think you are. It may seem the pain your marriage is causing you is the worst experience of your life—but could it be that God is setting you up for a new kind of wild marriage? Might it be that you don't have the power within *yourself* to create a happy marriage? Could it be that God has set you up to drown before you learn to swim? Could a God-wild marriage be the very thing you are longing for? Here's a checklist to see if you are ready for a wild, out-of-control marriage:

- *You have trouble connecting emotionally with your spouse.*
- *You know your spouse will not make you happy all the time.*
- *You know you can't make your spouse happy all the time.*
- *You know you don't know the future and can't control what may happen.*
- *You know circumstances change and you have little control over some events.*
- *You know you are limited in your power to forgive your spouse when he/she deeply hurts you.*
- *You know how difficult it is to love when your feelings aren't engaged.*
- *You've had lustful desires for other people outside of your marriage, and you are often unable to control those desires.*
- *You have experienced the loneliness of rejection and don't know how to handle it.*
- *You often feel helpless and have no idea how to build and maintain a joyful home.*

If any of these are true in your marriage, you are ready for Paul's admonition to us in Ephesians. You are ready to forge ahead into the God-centered, wild marriage you were created to experience.

Paul has written in depth about the nature of God and the church at the beginning of his letter (Ephesians 1-4) and is now concluding his challenge with practical, relational spirituality that is edgy, earthy, and daily. Paul is taking his readers into their marriage, home, and parenting life (Ephesians 5:18-6:4) like no other passage in the Bible. Paul wants his readers in Ephesus to clearly understand that the message he's bringing is not from the ivory towers of Gamaliel's school of Jewish systematic theology or the Sanhedrin Rules for Higher Living, but rather the pragmatic overflow of a personal, relational, growing, robust friendship with Jesus Christ.

THE BEGINNING IS THE END

It was T.S. Eliot who said, "In my end is my beginning."[15] We begin a journey by first deciding our destination. We must know our end before we begin. All endings take precedence over beginnings.

It is my presupposition from study, reflection, prayer, marriage counseling, and years of marriage that the only beginning that ends well is the beginning of knowing, praising, and loving God. We don't begin with "I want to have a happy marriage," or "I hope to be married twenty years from now," or "If I can have a fulfilling marriage and family, I shall be happy." As noble as each of these statements might sound, they all miss the end and thus, the beginning. Rather, marriage begins with God, the glory of God. Eugene Peterson writes,

> *"The end of all Christian life and obedience ... marriage and family ... the living of everything we know about God: life, life, and more life. But if we don't know where we are going, any road will get us there. But if we have a destination—in this case a life lived to the glory of God—there is a well-marked way, the Jesus-revealed Way."*[16]

We must begin our discussion with the Jesus-revealed Way, with His power, with His glory over your marriage and home.

Paul begins with this end in mind: "Do not be drunk with wine, but be filled with the Spirit." (Ephesians 5:18) It isn't the depersonalized techniques and skills you've learned or books you've read that make the difference. If this were the key, the U.S. would have the most amazing and effective marriages in the world! There are more conferences and books available for Christian marriage than ever before. No, the beginning questions are these: Who will be in control of your home? Who will rule over your marriage?

The vigor, spontaneity, and the playful freedom of real living can only come through the God-revealing Holy Spirit being invited into our lives. God wants to be in on your marriage. God wants to be in on your daily life and to take over, empower, energize, and bring vigor to your living. A sonnet by the poet and priest Gerard Manley Hopkins captures the Spirit of God alive in the human life.

> *I say more: the just man justices;*
> *Keeps grace: that keeps all his goings graces;*
> *Acts in God's eye what in God's eye he is—*
> *Christ. For Christ plays in ten thousand places,*
> *Lovely in limbs, and lovely in eyes not his*
> *To the Father through the features of men's faces.*[17]

Hopkins captures the Spirit of Christ that so desires to be revealed in every aspect of our lives. This is the God who wants to be revealed as behind, before, and above, but hidden within all details of our lives. Notice in Hopkins' poem the central verb is "plays." This verb captures the joy and freedom that the Holy Spirit desires for our lives. Jesus wants to "play" out His life of exuberance, grace, mercy, and wildness through our breathing, in our homes, in our workplaces, and through the most important aspect of our lives—our marriage relationships.

INTIMACY: SPIRIT TO SPIRIT

The God-wild marriage is an energized, robust union of our human spirit with God's Holy Spirit. It is the true intention of creation to be in intimacy with God and with our spouse through the power of God's Spirit. Adam "walked with God" in the garden by first having God breathe His own breath into him (Genesis 2). God the Father breathed His breath of Spirit dynamism into Adam's nostrils, and it was in this perfect Spirit-filled state that Adam "knew Eve." (Note: the word for "knowing" in the Old Testament Hebrew has the meaning of the deepest level of intimacy and the sexual relationship.) The first marriage began with the filling, breathing, empowering of the Holy Spirit. The triune intimacy of God through the infilling of His breath launched the first marriage.

Adam came alive through the breath of God. The Father breathed His life, His character, into Adam, and he became the "imageo Dei," the image of God, the imprint of God, the likeness of God to Eve. The uniqueness of Adam above all creation was the breath of God entering into him. William Law once wrote, "True Christianity is nothing but the continual dependence upon God through Christ for all life, light, and virtue; and the false religion of Satan is to seek that goodness from any other source."[18] All virtue, goodness, forgiveness, and peace come only through God's Spirit flowing within the Jesus follower. All deep eternal wisdom, knowledge, and insight must come from the wisdom of God revealed in the spirit of man. Jesus said,

> "I am the Real vine ... live in Me. Make your home in Me just as I do in you. In the same way that a branch can't bear grapes by itself but only by being joined to the vine, you can't bear fruit unless you are joined with Me. I am the Vine, you are the branches. When you're joined with me and I with you, the relation intimate and organic, the harvest is sure to be abundant. Separated, you can't produce a thing."[19] (John 15:1-7, The Message)

The divine power to live an adventurous, fruitful, wildly loving life does not come from our natural faculties. We must be joined to the Vine. We must be at home in Christ through an intimate relationship in which His life, His power, and His strength pours into us.

I enjoy fly fishing. There are several rivers in Colorado that I fish, located deep in canyons along crag-filled cliffs. Due to the rugged terrain around the river, I have to park my truck a good distance away. The parking area where I pull on my waders and boots is dusty, dry, and arid. Only sagebrush, piñon pine, and cactus can be found growing near the road. But as I walk the trail into the canyon, the arid atmosphere gives way to the humidity and fertile moisture of the swiftly moving river below. And suddenly the terrain is transformed into the wild beauty of budding dogwoods, vibrant columbine, and large, deeply rooted oak trees. The river has energized the landscape with its power and fertility.

Without the river, there is no life. With the river, all forms of vitality and fruitfulness pour forth. And so it is with our lives when we tap into the life-giving Spirit. Jesus said, "If anyone thirsts, let him come to me and drink. Rivers of living water will brim and spill out of the depths of anyone who believes in me ..." (John 7:37-39, *The Message*). He said this in regard to the Spirit, whom those who believed in him were about to receive. It is through the river of God, the Spirit of God, that our lives can brim over with the character and purposes of God.

Our lives without the intimacy of the Spirit are a dusty, arid terrain. You cannot in your own power have a consistently joyful marriage! It's impossible. You don't have the life and power in and of yourself. You can't change yourself, and you are powerless to change your spouse.

We've been taught since childhood that the route to happiness in anything we do is through *retaining* control — finding that supposedly free and peaceful place of being in control of our lives. But the

Bible teaches that the opposite is true: Your needs are best met when you release control. And this is nowhere truer than in the marriage relationship. We must give up control to the Holy Spirit. We must relinquish our needs and wants to God. We must quit demanding our rights and surrender to God's anointed power.

SURRENDER TO GOD'S CONTROL

We return to Paul's opening sentence, "And do not be drunk with wine, in which is dissipation; but be filled with the Spirit ..." (Ephesians 5:18). This opening verse to Paul's discussion of the marriage relationship emphasizes the first step—for without this beginning we will never have the power to live the God-wild marriage. Notice that Paul is not *suggesting* this beginning. No, instead he uses the imperative command form: Paul is *commanding* us to give our life, love, and destiny over to Jesus the liberator, to the wild Jesus Who has the power to break off our chains of selfishness and pride. Paul is relying on the strongest form of the Greek language to charge us to be filled with the addiction-breaking, chain-smashing, freedom-giving Jesus. It all starts and ends here! If we don't get this, forget the rest.

You may know Jesus as the Salvation Giver, but have you experienced Him as the Power Supplier? Do you have the power of Jesus in your marriage and home? After almost thirty years of ministry in counseling and helping couples, I've found that most "Christian couples" don't have a legitimate clue what this verse means. They are convinced that they are saved from hell when they die and are going to heaven because they've "prayed the prayer," but they're living in hell on earth because the power of the gospel, the power of Jesus, has never really invaded their day-to-day lifestyle and marriage. Are you living a kind of hell on earth right now? Have you discovered the power of being filled with the Holy Spirit? Have you let Jesus reign and rule in your life? Have you surrendered to the grace of God and allowed His love to flow into your relationship with your spouse?

To experience the God-wild marriage of passion and love you must give up control to Jesus, through the power of the Holy Spirit. You must release your power to control your marriage and spouse to the Holy Spirit. You must die, give up, and release your life, so that He can live, take over, and reveal His power and love to you.

If you are a Jesus follower, you already have the Holy Spirit living within you. In John 3, Jesus says, "Unless one is born of water and the Spirit, he cannot enter the kingdom of God." (John 3:5) In other words, you must be born physically and spiritually to enter into salvation. The Spirit of God enters into us when we believe in Christ. When we trust in Christ, the Spirit of God comes and seals us for salvation. Paul writes, "In Him you also trusted, after you heard the word of truth, the gospel of your salvation; in whom also, having believed, you were sealed with the Holy Spirit of promise." (Ephesians 1:13) Thus, upon believing in Jesus, you receive the Holy Spirit and are baptized and engrafted into God. We have the triune God (Father, Son, and Holy Spirit) living in our hearts, but that doesn't mean you are filled with and empowered by the Holy Spirit.

As a follower of Jesus, you have the same source of power that created the heavens and the earth residing within your life! The same Jesus Who healed the sick, caused blind eyes to see, and raised people from the dead, lives within your heart. And He wants that same life of power in your marriage. But until you daily die to yourself and daily live to Christ, you will not have this power ruling in your life.

Paul begins with, "And do not be drunk with wine ..." He is drawing upon a metaphorical comparison that those reading his letter would have understood. Getting drunk would have been a regular experience for the Ephesians before they became followers of Jesus. He is addressing a people who had been addicted to the intoxicating influences of the Temple of Artemis in Ephesus, at the time considered one of the seven wonders of the ancient world. Looming over the whole city, the temple would have been one of its most prominent structures.

At the Temple of Artemis, "worshippers" came and experienced ecstatic religious experiences through fermented drink that brought on visions and hallucinations that were considered messages from the gods. In the *IVP Bible Background Commentary*, Craig S. Keener writes:

> *"Many people in the ancient world believed that drunkenness could produce a sort of inspiration or possession by Dionysus, god of wine. Dionysus's most active worshipers yielded control of themselves to him and performed sexual acts or acts full of sexual symbolism."*[20]

So these recently converted disciples of Jesus understood power, even supernatural power. The Ephesians had firsthand experience in giving over control of their bodies to other powers.

Several years ago, our family purchased a new stereo system but could not get it to work. I turned the knobs and pushed all the right buttons, but still it had no sound. I was about ready to repack the stereo and return it to the store, when out of the blue one of my children suggested we plug the stereo into the electrical outlet! This must be why God gave us kids. Embarrassed and humbled, but laughing, I plugged in the stereo, and guess what? It worked. (Amazing what electrical power can do for an electrically powered instrument.) All of the electrical power of southern Colorado was flowing into our home, but without being connected, it did us no good. Likewise, the filling of the Holy Spirit connects us to all the spiritual power of the universe. To be filled with the Spirit is to be "plugged into" God's supernatural power.

SOMETHING MORE

Most believers in Christ have a "salvation relationship" but not a "Spirit-filled relationship" with Jesus. They are not empowered daily with God's Spirit. I repeat, not filled with the Spirit. The filling of the Holy Spirit is much more than just believing in Jesus, reading the Bible, and attending church. It's about allowing our lives to be filled up with all the fullness and fruitfulness of God — to be "plugged into" the spiritual power we have from Christ. Paul writes to the Ephesians, "For this reason I bow my knees to the Father of our Lord Jesus Christ ... that you may be filled with all the fullness of God." (Ephesians 3:14-19) The fullness of God is the love and acceptance of Jesus flowing through you. It's living out the Gospel. It's living daily in the power and fullness of Jesus.

The Spirit-filled life is about being controlled, directed, and empowered by Jesus Christ. Ultimately, Jesus wants total control; Jesus wants all of your heart and mind. A.W. Tozer wrote, "Though every believer has the Holy Spirit, the Holy Spirit does not have every believer." Does the Spirit have you? Will you let Him have your marriage? This is the foundation for the God-wild marriage — God takes over; you give up control.

Jesus is wildly in love with you. He has not given you just the ABC's for love's salvation, but the A to Z for love's sanctification — the trans- formation of your lifestyle. The liberation of love in our hearts begins with the Gospel, the love of Jesus. Everything in our life rises and falls on who is controlling our love life. The solution to marriage is the reorientation of our love life. This might sound a bit radical, but love in our marriage is not in directing more love toward our spouse, but rather focusing more of our attention on just how loved we are by Jesus.

The Spirit-empowered life is coming to the full realization that you are wildly loved by a wild God who wants you to daily experience a wild adventure with Him that will overflow into your relationship with your spouse.

PREACH JESUS TO YOURSELF

Jesus accepted you and me not because we had our act together and behaved perfectly; rather, He fully accepted us in spite of our selfishness and rebellion; He loves us because of our sin. We will never be good enough for God's love, but we certainly are bad enough. You will see later as I discuss Ephesians 5:25 in Chapter 4, He is the ultimate spouse to us, and He is the solution to our unfaithfulness, our stinginess.

Jesus is faithful. Jesus is generous. We are not.

The Spirit-filled life is reorienting our lives around Who Jesus is. It is preaching the Gospel to yourself.

The Spirit-filled life is the Gospel-filled life, the Jesus-filled life—the grace-filled life! Simply put, we must keep preaching the Gospel to ourselves that Jesus went to the cross for our sins and rose from the dead to set us free. When we do this, we experience God's truth that we are fully loved, accepted, and healed in Christ.

For many, that might not seem like the best way to make progress—I have heard people say, "Wait, you are saying that the first step to a happy marriage is to grow in Christ by telling myself how graciously loved I am? That doesn't seem like incentive enough. I need something to obey." Good point, bad theology. Because most of us have grown up with a religion of fear, we needed something to obey—something that if not obeyed, might mean God won't answer our prayers or take us to Heaven.

The God-wild life teaches us that the sheer grace of God has saved us from Hell and delivered us from sin. The God-wild life reveals to our hearts and minds that Jesus is the chain-breaker, the liberator, the giver of grace in our lives. This Liberator, Jesus, wants to have full access into every realm of our life and marriage. This is vital to our understanding: If you don't personally experience this wildly extravagant grace through Jesus, you absolutely won't find it in your spouse.

THE MAIN PURPOSE OF MARRIAGE

No other part of our life requires so much from us as marriage. There is frustration and seemingly impossible challenges. Could it be that this *is* the point—the purpose of marriage? Could it be that one of God's purposes for marriage is to make us realize we have to depend on Him? Might it be that Jesus put this other person in your life because it would force you to need more of Him? In *The Transformation of the Inner Man*, John and Paula Sandford express this powerfully, writing, "God gives us a beloved enemy [spouse] to force us spiritually lazy people to face what is undealt with in our flesh, else we would go through life ever congratulating ourselves that we are okay without Him."[21] Could it be that the God of the universe, knowing that we would never be able to produce the power to love that other person in and of ourselves, gave us marriage as the tool to press us into needing Him? Gary Thomas said it this way:

> *"Any situation that calls me to confront my selfishness has enormous spiritual value ... the real purpose of marriage may not be happiness as much as it is holiness. Not that God has anything against happiness, or that happiness and holiness are by nature mutually exclusive, but looking at marriage through the lens of holiness began to put it into an entirely new perspective for me."[22]*

Marriage shows us our lack of power and our need for the gospel of love and acceptance more than any other area of our life.

It's like the Dell laptop I used for years. It was a 2002 version with all the space and power needed in 2002. It even had the memory and power to get me all the way up to 2007. But in 2008 it became apparent to our IT department that the freezes and slowdowns (it was taking about ten minutes just to start) were due in large part to the lack of power and space I needed for the new programs I was now using. It was not a *bad* computer, but I could not expect more power than it was designed to give. I needed a more powerful computer.

I'll never forget the moment God spoke to me about power in our marriage. Liz and I had just had another one of those fun "discussions" that ended up looking like the Ultimate Fighting Championships—so I took a walk. Ladies, guys do two things after a fight: They go work in the garage, or they go for a walk. (Some punch the wall, but I wouldn't recommend this unless you are a doctor or contractor.) I stepped outside to walk and pray. As I shared my heart with the Lord and cried out to Him for strength, I was not expecting what I heard in my spirit. God spoke to me and said, "Steve, this marriage is not about Liz. It's about you. I've given her to you to change you, from the inside out." Wow. Not exactly what I wanted to hear.

THE 24/7 WORKOUT

God has given you marriage as His gymnasium for working out a new kind of you—that part of you that must surrender to God's love and power, which is the ultimate test of the gospel in our lives. 1 Timothy 4:7 exhorts us to "train yourself to be godly." The word for "train," *gumnos,* is the root word from which we derive the English word *gymnasium.* Marriage is God's gymnasium for working out holiness in our lives. This is the daily Spirit-filled life. Ruth Bell Graham, in being interviewed about her marriage to evangelist Billy Graham, said, "The problem with being married to Billy is that it's just so daily." Marriage is a 24-hours-a-day, seven-days-a-week spiritual workout. Don't you wish you could lose five pounds every time you showed love to your spouse?

The Christian life is also communal. The Bible is clear: Jesus did most of His teaching at parties and feasts. Jesus lived his last three years twenty-four/seven with twelve disciples. Adam and Eve were created into a communal relationship with each other, and Heaven, you remember, is depicted as a feast. Marriage is the community God designed for us to experience the gospel because we know ourselves best in community (the opposite of what our individualistic maverick-driven culture tells us). We will never know Jesus deeper than through community. Without relational accountability and communal struggles for forgiveness and understanding, we can't know Jesus deeply. This is the "why" of the church, and the "why" of marriage: community. We who are married will never know Jesus and His power and love outside of the community of marriage.[23]

Marriage is the central community God uses as the crucible of life that challenges everything within our character and soul. Marriage calls us to a new level of selfless living that is antagonistic to everything within our natural inclinations. Mort Fertel, a recognized authority on relationships, said, "Sustaining love is not a passive or spontaneous experience. It'll never just happen to you. You can't 'find' lasting love. You have to 'make' it day in and day out. That's why we have the expression 'the labor of love.'"[24] Marriage takes every fiber of our heart and mind to force us to rise to a new level of love and forgiveness, an action that is naturally impossible.

So, here is the reason Paul writes in our passage that we are to "be" filled with the Spirit. Grammatically, the phrase means "to be being," or "continuous action." The condition implies that being filled with the Spirit does not stop with an initial experience, but is maintained daily through the action of "be *being* filled." The *Wycliffe Commentary* defines it well: "Keep on being filled; be continuously filled with the Spirit. A believer can never obtain more of the Holy Spirit, for he indwells the Christian's life in all his fullness. But the Holy Spirit can get more of the believer; that is, he can exercise complete control of the life that is yielded to him."

It is what Christian writer Francis de Sales wrote about in the seventeenth century. While giving spiritual guidance to a young woman about the value of marriage, he wrote, "The state of marriage is one that requires more virtue and constancy than any other. It is a perpetual exercise of mortification ... From this thyme plant, in spite of the bitter nature of its juice, you may be able to draw and make honey of a holy life."[25] Notice he uses the words "bitter" and "honey" in the same sentence.

Marriage is bittersweet. To get to the sweet, we most often have to pray and surrender through the bitter. To spiritually grow through marriage, we must squeeze the honey out through the bitter juice as we navigate the labyrinth of a growing relationship with our Lord and our spouse. Without Jesus and His power, this is impossible.

Yes, there is bitter juice in every marriage. But God has given us the power of His Holy Spirit to draw out honey from the marriage plant. The greatest resource for living the God-wild marriage is the reality that it can only be done through God's power, not our own.

ARE YOU BOLD ENOUGH?

It is my premise that most couples want a great marriage, but they are not bold enough to go after it! It takes passion to get passion. They settle for a bland, boring, and tame relationship. But if we will just think about the gospel of Jesus—the unblushing promises of God, the unparalleled rewards of God's acceptance and grace—we would be more bold and aggressive in seeking His plan and purposes. God designed marriage to change us, to transform us more into the likeness of His love, His forgiveness, His image. Jonathan Edwards, the great Puritan preacher, once commented that very family should be a little church. God wants your marriage and your family to be a venue for His glory and image to shine out to the world.

Jesus wants your marriage to reflect the kingdom of God and His joy. Jesus was boldly happy and joyful (why do you think the Pharisees criticized him so much for partying and hanging out with sinners?) and He wants our lives to be full of His glory and joy. It is as we are daily filled with Jesus that we begin to look like Him in our marriage. Don't you want more than you are currently experiencing? Jesus wants to fill your marriage with His love, His forgiveness, and His infinite joy. The great Oxford professor C.S. Lewis in a sermon titled "The Weight of Glory," writes:

> If there lurks in most modern minds the notion that to desire our own good and earnestly to hope for the enjoyment of it is a bad thing, I submit that this notion has crept in from Kant and the Stoics and is no part of the Christian faith. Indeed, if we consider the unblushing promises of reward and the staggering nature of the rewards promised in the Gospels, it would seem that Our Lord finds our desires not too strong, but too weak. We are half-hearted creatures, fooling about with drink and sex and ambition when infinite joy is offered us, like an ignorant child who wants to go on making mud pies in a slum because he cannot imagine what is meant by the offer of a holiday at the sea. We are far too easily pleased.

We are far too easily pleased with our lives of selfish pleasures and self-empowered marriages. Jesus wants to rule and reign over your marriage. He wants you to experience a God-wild, Spirit-empowered marriage filled with His mission, His heart, His joy, through surrendering your relationship with your spouse completely to Him. Jesus, in being quizzed by a lawyer about the greatest commandment in the Law, replied, "'You shall love the Lord your God with all your heart, with all your soul, and with all your mind.' This is the first and great commandment. And the second is like it: 'You shall love your neighbor as yourself.' On these two commandments hang all the Law and the Prophets." (Matthew 22:36-40) In other words, our love for God directly depends on our love for our neighbor, and your closest neighbor is sleeping next to you each night. You prove your love for God by loving your spouse.

INVITE JESUS INTO YOUR MARRIAGE

Have you ever invited Jesus into your marriage? I'm not just talking about an individual prayer for your own salvation, but a communal prayer for sanctification. (If you haven't ever fully surrendered your life to Christ, now would be a good time.) Have you given Jesus control of your marriage and family through the filling of the Holy Spirit?

When I first met Liz, I was knocked over by her physical beauty. Her walk, her voice, her body, and her hair really turned me on. From the moment I met Liz, every other girl was compared to her. She was the new standard. But as we got to know each other more, what kept drawing me toward her was her heart and passion for Jesus and commitment to Him. Liz had a wild, extravagant desire to live for God. When we were dating, we spent hours at a time discussing what God was showing us in our relationships with Him. We were and still are bound together through our common trust and vision for Jesus.

But most marriages don't begin this way. Most people don't begin with the vision of letting Jesus rule and reign in their relationship with each other. That may be true in your marriage. You may not have started out your marriage with Jesus front and center, but you can begin now. Kneel down and invite Jesus to take over your marriage right now. Don't wait another day.

This is not a once-for-all-time prayer, but must be repeated daily. Yes, daily. Begin this week to pray together as a couple, and commit to doing so at least once a week. The filling and power of the Holy Spirit is an intimate relationship that continually gives control over to Jesus, allowing Him to rule in our hearts. The power comes from God, but it must be engaged through surrender every day. Give up control. Die to yourself and let Jesus take over! You'll never regret it. The rest of this book depends on this decision. Without the power of Jesus flowing in your marriage, everything else we're about to talk about will be impossible.

Conversation Starters

Up to this point, who or what has been controlling your marriage? Why?

If Jesus, through the power of the Holy Spirit, were to take control of your marriage, what kind of a difference would it make?

Will you give Jesus control of your marriage? If so, will you as an individual or couple kneel down and give your marriage, your relationship with each other, over to God?

Will you commit to praying together at least once a week? If so, you are inviting supernatural power into your marriage! Be bold!

CHAPTER 2:
SHOUTING ALOUD ALLOWED

While God is everywhere, He is not everywhere manifested. He is most "at home" in praise and, being at home, He manifests Himself best as God. When you or I choose to make God at home through praise, we invite Him to act "at home."

Jack Taylor

... speaking to one another in psalms and hymns and spiritual songs, singing and making melody in your heart to the Lord, giving thanks always for all things to God the Father in the name of our Lord Jesus Christ.

Ephesians 5:19-20

I was hanging out with my seven-year-old son, Josh, one day by a campfire when he said, "Daddy, is my voice going to change one day?"

"Yes, it is," I replied.

"Why?" he asked.

As I was pondering exactly how much of the testosterone tale I needed to tell him at his tender age, he very excitedly announced:

"Well, when *my* voice changes, I'm going to speak Japanese!"

We have four children who have passed through the unsettling, often-conflicted years childhood experts call "adolescence." If you're a parent, you know how crazy those years can be. Of the many physiological changes during this time, one of the more dramatic (to the child) and humorous (to parents) is the voice change. You know it's happening to your son when you call home and a man whom you've never met answers the phone. You know your boy is changing when, as he sings to the song on the radio, he tries to hit those high notes and it sounds like he just got hit by a truck.

But we all know that the changing of our child's voice is a sign of growth and maturity. Pediatricians tell us that the voice box is a structure at the top of the windpipe that is made of cartilage. Stretched across it are two vocal cords, which are a bit like elastic bands. As air is expelled from the lungs, it passes between the vocal cords, making them vibrate. As a young boy grows, testosterone increases in the body, causing the cartilage to grow larger and thicker. During adolescence, the vocal cords also thicken and grow 60 percent longer. Now when they vibrate, they do so at a lower frequency than before. With the release of more testosterone, the facial bones grow, creating bigger spaces within the face. Larger cavities in the sinuses, nose, and back of the throat give the voice more room in which to resonate, thus deepening the voice further. Even though we may laugh whenever our kid's voice breaks or croaks, we know this is the natural result of a gradually maturing body. It's not only natural, but healthy. A healthy child will grow physically, and with growth will come a tonal change to one's voice.

In a similar way, as we mature in giving control of our lives and marriages to Jesus, through the power of the Holy Spirit, our voices will also change. God wants our tongues! God wants to have what is admittedly the most difficult area of our life to control—our tongue, our communication with Him and with our spouse. But this is difficult—especially in the marriage relationship.

27 MINUTES A WEEK?

One researcher found that "the average married couple actively communicates on the average of just twenty-seven minutes a week."[27] Unbelievably, most couples "exchange the most words on their third date and the year before a divorce."[28] Most marriages rise and fall on the use, lack of use, misuse, and abuse of the tongue. Obviously most couples are not communicating very well. (But they are shopping. The average married couple shops six hours a week!)

Communication is risky. The experts say how a couple communicates, how they use their tongues with each other (I know what you're thinking, but that's not what I'm talking about—wait for Chapter 6), is one of the most important indicators of a happy or unhappy marriage. In *Twelve Hours to a Great Marriage*, the authors list several verbal "risk factors" that can most damage a relationship:

- *having negative styles of talking and arguing (for example, putting each other down, refusing to talk, or yelling)*
- *having a hard time communicating, especially when you disagree*
- *not being able to handle disagreements* [29]

These risk factors are the ingredients in a simmering brew of eventual marital misery and disaster.[30] But it is in learning to tame our impulsive tongues and intentionally expressing our hearts in more positive and loving ways that we can see God transform our dying, atrophying marriages into great ones.

SURRENDERING YOUR HEART AND TONGUE

Just after his command to be filled with the Holy Spirit, Paul provides us with the first indicator, the first step into the Jesus-honoring, wild, Spirit-empowered marriage by saying, "speaking to one another in psalms and hymns and spiritual songs, singing and making melody in your heart to the Lord, giving thanks always for all things to God the Father in the name of our Lord Jesus Christ." (Ephesians 5:19-20)

Marriage turns into a God-wild adventure when a couple is growing in surrendering their tongues to the Lord. When God gets our hearts, He also gets our mouths. When the early church was first empowered with the Holy Spirit at Pentecost, the most obvious change was in their speech. What caught the attention of the people that gathered that day was "we hear them telling in our own tongues the mighty works of God." (Acts 2:11) Praise poured forth from the early followers of Jesus as they were filled with the Holy Spirit.

The greatest evidence of the Spirit-empowered life was in the use of their tongues through praise to God. Their tongues were transformed from fear to faith, from worry to worship (Acts 1-2). And between then and now, nothing has changed. When individuals and couples learn to give over to God their lives and surrender control of their marriages *and speech* to Jesus, He will fill our mouths with praise.

The Bible tells us that our tongue is an extension of our heart. We literally *hear* someone's heart. The words they choose and the attitude they have are reflections of how they are feeling or what they are believing in their hearts. On any given day, I can tell how Liz is doing emotionally just by talking to her on the phone. How she answers my call, with just one sentence, tells me 90 percent of what I need to know about her heart state.

Jesus explained it this way: "For out of the abundance of the heart the mouth speaks." (Matthew 12:34b) The attitudes and beliefs of our hearts dictate and create the words formed in our mouths. As go the attitudes of our hearts, so go the words of our mouths, so go our entire lives. James, the brother of Jesus and a leader in the early church, gives us God's stark analysis of the tongue by comparing it to a horse's bridle or a ship's rudder:

> *For we all stumble in many things. If anyone does not stumble in word, he is a perfect man, able also to bridle the whole body. Indeed, we put bits in horses' mouths that they may obey us, and we turn their whole body. Look also at ships: although they are so large and are driven by fierce winds, they are turned by a very small rudder wherever the pilot desires. (James 3:2-4)*

A person who can control his tongue can control every area of his life! An individual who can control his tongue can control the atmosphere of his/her marriage and family. I know this is true. As a pastor, my words are under the scrutiny of thousands of people each week. And I blow it all the time. If I make a mistake in a statement, there is someone who will notice, and when Monday rolls around, the emails come flooding in. My choice of words directs an entire church. My choice of words creates a negative or positive atmosphere *in* our church.

Your words to your spouse create joy or anxiety. The tongue is a rudder that directs the ship on the atmospheric sea of attitudes in your marriage. God created the tongue to impact other lives. This is precisely why the power of the Holy Spirit filling a life begins His greatest and deepest work by taking over our tongues.

PRAISE LEVERAGE

The Greek philosopher Archimedes once said, "Give me a place to stand, and I will move the world." I'm not exactly sure what Archimedes meant, but I suspect he was speaking about leverage. Leverage requires three things. First, there needs to be a point of leverage, and second, there must be a lever. Third, the lever must be pushed against a fulcrum to move something. In relation to our marriages, praise undoubtedly is the lever, the sovereignty of God is the point of leverage, and *we* must make the choice to move—to initiate and fill our lives with praise.[31]

So what is praise? Praise is adoration of God that is audible, active, assertive, and demonstrative.[32] This is exactly what Paul is saying. He admonishes us to go about "speaking to one another in psalms and hymns and spiritual songs, singing ..." Praise is the audible expression of our love for God. Praise is the result of experiencing God's truth in our lives.

Praise is the leverage that releases the Holy Spirit to work in our marriage. Praise takes our hearts and minds off of our circumstances, troubles, and issues, and opens us up to new possibilities in Christ. The Bible makes such audacious statements as "with God all things are possible" (Matthew 10:27) — and when a couple learns to praise God, they open themselves up to powerful possibilities for transformation and new life. The God-wild marriage is a God-wild adventure to learning to fill your home with praise!

Years ago, while living in Japan, Liz and I were faced with a situation that was of deep concern to us. We didn't know what to do. No human answers were working. It was one of those circumstances that we all face from time to time, where there are not any clear answers, and the whole thing feels overwhelming. Even after prayer and discussion with friends, we did not feel any peace or closure. It was at this point of frustration that we decided as a couple that we needed a time of praise and prayer each day to get us through this difficult time.

It was awkward at first (doing spiritual things as a couple always is) and we didn't really know exactly what we were doing. We had a lot of Christian couple friends and didn't know anyone who spent time worshipping together. We were on our own. I can't sing, and it must have been torture for Liz — but we wanted God's glory, God's power, and God's presence over our home. So, we began gathering together as a couple every night to sing praises, hymns, and spiritual songs to the Lord. We used our little Japanese-made stereo and just sang along with worship songs. We used a hymnal and sang some of the old favorites of the church. After singing, we would pray. We did something different each week. And what began as awkward and self-conscious became God-focused, and we forgot about how we sounded or looked as we experienced God's sovereign joy and truth.

And guess what? God showed up! God's presence and power began to fill our home with faith, joy, and fresh peace. God came powerfully into what seemed like an impossible situation. It was amazing. It was wildly surprising. We could feel God's presence and anointing over our home like never before in our married life. We experienced answers to our prayers as we sought Him. It was as if the power of God was unleashed over our marriage because of praise. Issues that had before taken long periods of time to grapple with in our marriage seemed to be resolved more quickly and with more wisdom.

What began as a little experiment took on a life of its own. Praise does that. Praise and the presence of God took over our marriage and our home. As the years have passed, Liz and I, and now our children joining us, have learned the presence and power of God in our marriage and home through the regular practice of praise and prayer. We have sought God through praise and prayer for our finances, our disagreements, our parenting, our plans, and our sex life. (Yes, I did say that!) With every challenge and every failure (and we've had plenty), we have made praise and worship our routine. Praise and prayer have transformed our marriage and home. Praise has proven to be the avenue for God's power to be released over our marriage and family!

GOD'S LIVING ROOM

I travel a lot. In the various hotels I've stayed in around the world, I have slept on tilted beds, confronted noisy drunks in the next room, tossed and turned in sweaty, sultry island humidity, slept under faulty mosquito netting, and scratched all night. Even though I've learned to put up with most inconveniences, I am most "at home," most comfortable and most relaxed, when I return to my own house in Colorado. I love sitting in my own special chair, with Gracie, my Labrador, cuddled up next to my feet, a hot mocha in hand, and a blazing fire in our fireplace. Nothing relaxes me more than being in my home, with my family, in my living room.

And God is most comfortable in *His* living room too. The last book of the Bible, Revelation, gives us a picture of what God enjoys in His living room. God invites John, the writer of this piece, to

"Come up here, and I will show you ..." (Revelation 4:1) This is the opportunity of a lifetime—to visit God's living room. John describes for us a massive, loud, extravagant praise and worship service! John describes to us what he sees: a glorious throne and One seated on this throne (Revelation 4:2), and around His throne are creatures that "day and night never cease to say, holy, holy, holy, is the Lord God Almighty, who was and is and is to come!" (v. 8)

Heaven is God's living room. The only place in all of reality that has no sin. No rebellion. No competition for God's complete control and sovereignty.

And God's living room is full of praise, prayers, and worship (read all of Revelation 4). God must be most comfortable in the atmosphere of praise and prayer because He has His own living room filled with it constantly and continually!

In Psalms 22:3 we read, "But You are holy, Enthroned in the praises of Israel." The word for "enthroned" is *yashab* and has the meaning of "sitting down; dwelling; or settling."[33] Praise is where God is most at home; it is where He is most "settled." Praise is God's home; it's His living room. It is in the atmosphere of praise that Jesus is most comfortable.

If you want to see Jesus revealed in your marriage, then make him feel "at home," in *your* home. Make your living room His living room. Because He is enthroned through your praise and prayer and is most comfortable and liberated to work through such an atmosphere, you can make your marriage a little bit like heaven (on earth) by practicing the habit of praise and prayer.

If praise—and as a result, our prayers—is only a collection of illusive hopes built on some exercise in positive thinking, then our faith will only be built on our own personal ability to drum up a feeling that will flee with each difficult circumstance. But if we believe that praise is the lever that moves the hand of Jesus in our marriage, then we are onto something entirely revolutionary! I believe that the wildly passionate, purposeful marriage is for those that learn the secret and discipline of praise. Why? Because praise releases God's manifest presence over our marriage. And you cannot experience all of the God-empowered, God-sustained marriage without God's presence.

Because God is omnipresent—meaning that He is present everywhere—I purposefully use the term "manifest presence." I'm making a distinction between God's omnipresence and His *manifest* presence. While God is everywhere present, He is not everywhere manifested. Though God is everywhere present with His Spirit, He is not always manifesting His presence. The manifest presence of God is when His Spirit comes in power and we can personally sense, and at times "feel," His peace and power in our lives. Praise releases God to manifest Himself to us. We desperately need God's manifest presence in our marriages!

God is most glorified in praise because praise is "nothing more or less than a commitment to, and a confession of, the sovereign power and providence of God."[34] And where God is most glorified, He is most present. Praise opens the door to God's manifest presence and lines our marriages up with what is happening in heaven. When we open the door of praise, we open up the door to God's home—and where God is most "at home," He best manifests Himself as God.

PRAISE DRIVES BACK DARKNESS

Have you figured out that there are enemy forces working all around you, committed to destroying your marriage? There are malevolent spirits, demons, who are attempting to infiltrate your marriage relationship (see Chapter 5) and drive a wedge of anger, bitterness, and isolation into your love life. There are enemies to our happiness driven by Satan, who are secretly (and not so secretly) worming their way into our lives in order to create discord and distrust. The goal of this darkness, these spirits, is division and destruction. Satan and demons know that if they can divide a couple, they can destroy the marriage.

A mouth filled with praise is a mouth filled with weapons for warfare! A marriage filled with praise is a weapon against the enemy. In Psalm 149:5-6 we read, "Let the godly exult in glory; let them sing for joy on their beds. Let the high praises of God be in their throats and two-edged swords in their hands." Praise has victory properties in the battle for our homes.

Praise changes the atmosphere of our hearts and our lives. Praise drives back the darkness, disunity, and disease of demons. We see the power of praise in an interesting story in the Bible found in 2 Chronicles 20. Jehoshaphat, king of Judah, one day realizes that a coalition of enemy nations from Moab, Ammon, and their auxiliaries have entered his country and surrounded Judah. Jehoshaphat is full of fear (2 Chronicles 20:3), and seeks God through prayer and fasting. God speaks to the king through one of the worship leaders to "not be afraid and do not be dismayed at this great horde, for the battle is not yours but God's." (v. 15)

It's what Jehoshaphat does next that is instructive. On the following day, the king appoints singers to lead the charge into battle — not with swords and chariots, but with praise. On the vanguard of Judah, headed straight into the mouth of the enemy, Jehoshaphat sends singers who are told to "give thanks to the Lord, for his steadfast love endures forever." (v. 21) and what does God do? "And when they began to sing and praise, the Lord set an ambush against the men of Ammon ... so that they were routed." (v. 22) The Hebrew word used here, *yadah*, means "giving thanks with hands extended." Thus, they entered into battle with praise, and God won the victory through a supernatural deliverance.

We see God's deliverance power again in Acts 16:25 when Paul and Silas are praising God at midnight while incarcerated in a Philippian jail. As they praise the Lord, God releases power. The Holy Spirit shows up in power through an earthquake, and the foundations of the prison are so shaken that the doors fly open!

Praise drives back the enemies of our marriage. It is a mystery that God has created praise for warfare and victory. In Psalm 8:2 we read, "From the children and infants you have ordained praise because of your enemies, to silence the foe and the avenger." The word for praise in this passage can be translated *strength*. "Praise" and "strength" can be used interchangeably. Jack Taylor writes of this passage:

> "The truth is that praise is strength and strength is praise. From the simple, the toddlers and babes, God appoints praise because, in its essence, it stops the enemy dead in his tracks! Neither the devil nor his demons can offer any protest after praise. They are hushed."[35]

Praise is a God-ordained weapon for driving back the schemes of the enemy in our marriage relationships. Praise breaks the power of demons by sending out the greater creative power of the Holy Spirit and the presence of God into our homes.

"PRAISE&PRAYER THERAPY"

It seems like everyone we know is in some kind of "therapy" these days. There is therapy for undereating, overeating, underachieving, overachieving, being undersexed and oversexed—you name it, there's a counselor who can help you. Let me propose Praise&Prayer Therapy.

Praise not only lifts up Jesus and opens the door for His manifest presence in our marriage, but also changes us. Paul says "...making melody in your heart to the Lord, giving thanks always for all things to God the Father in the name of our Lord Jesus Christ" (vs. 19b, 20). Praise is focused attention on God that exalts Jesus, but praise also does something to *our* hearts. A therapy for our souls. As praise bursts forth from our mouths, it transforms our thinking and soothes our spirit. Praise changes us! Praise changes our thinking, which changes our attitudes and actions.

Such praise opens up our minds to new-found faith in our prayers being answered. You can no more pray with faith without praise than eating without opening your mouth. Prayers pour forth with newly discovered trust as our hearts and minds are impacted through an attitude of praise and worship.

Most of us begin our marriages with great expectations of romance, companionship, and a growing friendship with our spouse. What begins so well often diminishes into sniper attacks on the other person's character, weaknesses, and personality. The very things that once drew us to the other person can often be what we attack the most. Then, our tongues become tools of destruction and negativity that diminish the other person and start to rule over our thinking.

Our marriages desperately need joy and gladness. Paul even says that praise involves "making melody in your heart to the Lord." The word used for "melody" is very interesting. It comes from the Greek word *psallo*, which is the root word for *psalmois*, or psalm. Paul is saying "make your heart into a psalm." What a powerful statement. Like no other part of Scripture, the Psalms capture the passion and vibrancy of God's wild heart. The Hebrew title for the Psalms is *Sepher Tehillim*, meaning "Book of Praises." And no other book of the Bible speaks of praise and joy with more frequency than the Psalms. Psalms 16:11 captures the heart of the book and brings insight: "You will show me the path of life; In Your presence is fullness of joy." Praise brings joy into our marriages.

In one recent survey, couples reported that joy had the greatest bearing on their overall marital satisfaction.[36] Remember the early days of your courtship and dating relationship? Do you remember laughing together? Did you act silly with each other? Probably joy was a big part of your budding relationship.

Now imagine last month. What was it like? Are you and your partner still enjoying each other? Are you regularly laughing and finding time for each other's companionship? Mark Twain once said,

"To get the full value of joy you must have somebody to divide it with." Poet T.S. Elliot once said, "Time you enjoyed wasting is not wasted time." Taking time for praise in your marriage will bring with it the presence of God, which will result in the fullness of joy.

After twenty-five years of marriage, I'm convinced that the atmosphere of joy is vital to sustained intimacy, communication, and life in a marriage. I'm also of the deepening conviction, especially as I counsel other couples, that praise with prayer is the most powerful tool God has given us for a marriage filled with joy. You need joy in your marriage. Praise&Prayer Therapy is joy sustaining.

If your marriage is missing joy, it might be time to begin to regularly praise the Lord as a couple. Believe me, I know this will be difficult—I hated the thought of praising God and spending time worshipping the Lord in front of my wife at home. But if you truly want joy as the atmosphere of your marriage, it is worth the risk.

Find your favorite praise CD, log onto iTunes, or get out a hymnal and take time weekly (and if you're a wild risk-taker, daily) to worship the Lord. Start with just two songs, then pray together. Set up a time each week. Is this too wild? It probably is, but that's what this challenge is all about—going after God's joy. I told you this would be uncomfortable—all new habits are.

The wild God of the universe longs to enjoy our praise and hear our prayers. He wants *your* home to become *His* living room—a place of His presence and power! Start today. Go for it. *Carpe diem gloriae Dei*! (Seize the day for the glory of God!)

Conversation Starters

If you were to experience God's manifest presence in your marriage and in your home, what difference would it make?

Are you and your spouse practicing praise in your life? In your marriage? Why or why not?

What time each week can you come together for praise and prayer?

CHAPTER 3:
THE S-WORD

Submission is the divine calling of a wife to honor
and affirm her husband's leadership and help carry it through
according to her gifts.
John Piper

My Katie is in all things so obliging and pleasing to me that I
would not exchange my poverty for all the riches of Croesus.
Letter to Stifel from Martin Luther

... submitting to one another in the fear of God. Wives, submit
to your own husbands, as to the Lord. For the husband is head
of the wife, as also Christ is head of the church; and He is the
Savior of the body. Therefore, just as the church is subject to
Christ, so let the wives be to their own husbands in everything.
Ephesians 5:21-24

Several years ago, Liz and I had the privilege of watching the celebrated Israeli actor, Topol, perform live as Tevye in his stage masterpiece, *Fiddler on the Roof*, at the Pikes Peak Center in Colorado Springs. It was, to say the least, a stunning performance by one of the most talented actors of our generation.

The movie version of the play first hit the cinema in 1971 and was an instant blockbuster. The movie won three Oscars. Topol was nominated as Best Actor. Since that time Topol has played the role of Tevye over 2,500 times in stage performances around the world.

He has said in numerous interviews that "of all the stage performances" he's ever done, the role of Tevye is the one he was born to do. No one can play the part of Tevye quite like Topol. Of all the memorable dialogue, one of my favorite exchanges is between Topol and Mendel, the rabbi's son:

> Tevye: As Abraham said, "I am a stranger in a strange land…"
> Mendel: Moses said that.
> Tevye: Ah. Well, as King David said, "I am slow of speech, and slow of tongue."
> Mendel: That was also Moses.
> Tevye: For a man who was slow of tongue, he talked a lot.

What makes *Fiddler on the Roof* so meaningful? I believe it's the role of Tevye and his inner struggle to understand the changing culture in Russia at the turn of the century. Tevye, as father, provider, family sage, and village leader, is the role that makes the play work. The production team would agree—the original title of the play was not going to be *Fiddler on the Roof*, but *Tevye*.

But what would happen to the production if Topol wasn't allowed to play Tevye and instead had to play Mendel? What if, from time to time, Topol was asked to play Yente, the matchmaker? How ridiculous! What would be the result if each actor or actress could just decide to change characters and roles whenever they desired? Even in the middle of the production? The result would be chaos!

And chaos is the correct word to describe most marriages today! Most couples don't have a clue what role they are to play in a marriage relationship. The American culture has increasingly become androgynous. Men are told to act more feminine, and women are told be more masculine. The culture has told us for the past forty years that men need to "get in touch" with their feminine side and listen more and that women need to "wear the pants" in the home and be more assertive. There are aspects of the stereotypical man and woman in Western culture which have needed to change, and for those, we applaud. But the result, in many ways, has been role confusion, resulting in marriages in disarray.

This week I talked to a friend of mine who told me about the dissolution of his marriage—one that I once would have thought to be strong and vibrant. The conversation led into the particular counselor he and his wife had chosen during their time of difficulty. I knew from experience that this "Christian" counselor often pushed men hard about changing, but rarely—if ever—challenged the domain of the woman. With no biblical understanding of roles and the need for both genders to be transformed, he has brought great confusion into many marriages.

But God is not confused. In Ephesians 5, He is clearly spelling out that He has created divine roles and a divine order for the marriage. And these roles, if obeyed, can result in a marriage according to God's order that results in a wildly loving and exciting relationship. Dietrich Bonhoeffer, in writing about these roles, describes it as the "rule of life:"

> *God establishes a rule of life by which you can live together in wedlock: 'Wives, be subject to your husbands, as is fitting in the Lord. Husbands love your wives.' (Col 3:18,19) With your marriage you are founding a home. That needs a rule of life, and this rule of life is so important that God establishes it himself, because without it everything would be out of joint. You may order your home as you like, except in one thing: the wife is to be subject to her husband and the husband to love his wife.[37]*

Paul begins the introduction into our roles as husband and wife with one of the most dreaded words in the English language—the

S-word, submission. *"…submitting to one another in the fear of God. Wives, submit to your own husbands, as to the Lord."*

Let's be honest. Submission has a bad reputation! I've been in a lot of Christian book and gift shops and have yet to see a plaque with the words, "Submit to one another," or "Submit to your own husband." I've never, ever seen it. I doubt I ever will. Our perception of submission is of an "Archie Bunker husband" constantly railroading, manipulating, and making derogatory remarks to the "Edith" wife of his life—treating her as a doormat and bimbo, who hasn't a clue how to think on her own. Words like "doormat," "slave," and "clueless" come to mind. Our culture has bombarded us with a worldview that defines submission as inferiority.

But the misunderstanding flows both ways. Women not willing to surrender to Christ and their husbands' leadership, and also men unwilling to understand that submission cascades down through love and respect. I once had a man in my office who began our discussion about his poor marriage with the words, "If she would just submit like the Bible says, we wouldn't have all these problems. I'm the leader, and she needs to fall into line!" This is not the kind of attitude we're talking about.

A more twenty-first-century word that I would prefer to use is "support." Wives are called by God to support their husbands—in their jobs, their vision, finances, and childrearing. "Support" captures the spirit and meaning of Paul's letter.

WE ARE ALL EQUAL

The problem has been a postmodern, post-Christian culture that has increasingly defined roles in the home as either superior or inferior. (And not all for bad reasons. I'm not negating the fact that there are certainly men who abuse their role and women who have been deeply hurt by such chauvinism.) Yet our passage is not speaking of equality—the equality of the man and woman is a given. We are all created by God's design for a purpose, as children of God that are equal in His eyes. Paul makes our egalitarian status before God clear in his letter to the Galatians:

> *For you are all sons of God through faith in Christ Jesus. For as many of you as were baptized into Christ have put on Christ. There is neither Jew nor Greek, there is neither slave nor free, there is neither male nor female; for you are all one in Christ Jesus. (Galatians 3:26-28)*

The Bible is crystal clear that we are all created equal in God's eyes. Our gender is a gift from God, given sovereignly by God, and has no bearing on our worth before Him. When we place our faith in Christ as Savior and Lord, we are all, male or female, baptized into Christ with the same spiritual status. Regardless of our sex, we, as fellow followers of Jesus, are all one in Christ.

But, due to sin and the works of the devil, our culture and the church have redefined submission in ways never intended by God. John Piper notes, "It is a great sadness that in our society—even in the church—the different and complementary roles of biblical headship for the husband and biblical submission for the wife are despised or simply passed over."[38] Thus, let's look at what submission is *not* before we gaze into the beauty of what it was meant to be.

Submission is not:
- *Having no opinion of your own*
- *Having no say in making decisions and always agreeing with your husband*
- *Having to walk in fear of disagreeing with your husband*
- *Acquiescing to sinful choices knowingly made by your husband*
- *Allowing abusive behavior (whether physical, spiritual, or verbal)*

So what does submission mean? "Submission" in Greek is *hupotasso* and means "to place underneath, to be subject, to obey."[39] As Dr. George Knight III, dean and New Testament professor at Knox Theological Seminary, explains, "The meaning of *hupotasso*, used consistently in the charge to wives, is the same as its meaning in [Ephesians 5:21], that is submission in the sense of voluntarily yielding in love."[40] I love this definition of submission, "voluntarily yielding in love." It is as much an attitude as an action, involving both parties. Importantly, take note that verse 21 precedes verse 22: *submitting to one another in the fear of God. Wives, submit to your own husbands, as to the Lord.* The man has a responsibility to yield in love to the wife just as the woman yields to her husband. It is interesting that the mutual submission of the man and woman is dependent on a mutual submission "as to the Lord." In other words, we can't submit to one another without first submitting to Jesus.

JESUS AS OUR EXAMPLE

Submission — or the word I think better captures Paul's meaning, "support" — is a spiritual revolution that can only happen within our hearts when we surrender our life, our desires, and our passions to the Lord. The power of submission is the power of surrendering to Jesus. Every man and every woman who desires a God-wild marriage led and empowered by Jesus must learn the spirit of submission. Jesus Himself is our greatest example. His attitude of submission to his heavenly Father is our model in a marriage relationship. We are exhorted to have the same submitted attitude.

> *Let this mind be in you which was also in Christ Jesus, who, being in the form of God, did not consider it robbery to be equal with God, but made Himself of no reputation, taking the form of a bondservant, and coming in the likeness of men.* (Philippians 2:5-7)

Jesus yielded in love, obeyed, and served God the Father—even to the point of death on the cross. Submission is the DNA of the kingdom of God. The Triune God of the universe is in mutual submission to the roles given by God the Father. The Son submits to the Father; the Spirit submits to the Son. And we are called to submit to God, mutually, in our roles as husband and wife.

Paul is asking wives to submit to their husbands as their heads as the church submits to Christ as her head. In our next chapter, we will take the next step in Paul's progression—that of the husband loving his wife as Christ loved the church. A tall order, a deep order, but a divine order!

Liz has reminded me on many occasions that the admonition of Ephesians 5 only has three verses for women about submission, but *nine verses* instructing the man in how to love his wife! Some have said that men are a bit slower than women, and maybe God even agrees. In our next chapter I will take men into the journey of loving leadership, yet in verse 23 we read that "the husband is head of the wife, as also Christ is the head of the church, and He is the Savior of the body." The man indeed carries the weight of leading like Jesus! It does seem that in the same mysterious way in which Jesus leads His people, His church, we as men have been commissioned by God to a role of leading our wives—perhaps even saving our wives?

Men, could it be that the real reason we don't have wives who submit to our leadership is because we're not lovingly leading? Might it be that we haven't grasped the spiritual reality that Jesus has empowered us to lovingly lead as a kind of picture or type of salvation to our wives?

When men and women come into my office for marriage counseling, one of the first questions I have for the couple is, "Who's the spiritual leader of this home? Be honest." That's when the squirming and finger-pointing begins. Some of the more popular answers to my question are, "Well, no one!" or "If he would just love me, I'd submit!" or "She won't let me lead!" My response is "You're both just cowards! You don't really want Jesus in your marriage." That usually gets everyone mad, which is my first goal.

SUBBED TO A MISSION

My second question is usually, "What is the mission of your marriage?" This is a very important question, and it directly relates to submission. The English scholars who translated the Greek word *hupotasso* into the word "submission" captured the deep meaning of the word. Of the many English words they could have chosen, they picked "submission." Submission is a powerful word—it means to be "subbed," or under a "mission," a purpose, a vision, a calling! *Hupotasso* is a military term[41] that has the meaning of placing oneself under someone who has a mission. Submission literally, at its root, means to be following a mission, obeying a higher purpose, living for something greater than yourself.

Our passage says first of all that the man and woman, the husband and wife, are *both* to be "submitting to one another in the fear of God ..." That means they are both to be under God's mission, living underneath God's purpose! So, submission is for both the husband and the wife to be under God's purpose and plan, obeying Him, striving to live for Him. When you have a couple who have both yielded in love to Jesus, and are being filled with His Spirit daily, you will begin to experience the God-wild marriage for which you were created!

Yet then, the challenge is given to the woman to be in "sub" "mission" to the husband. *Wives, submit to your own husbands, as to the Lord.* What is God saying to us? Let me be frank. God is instructing us that the man is called to the role of leading his wife through and toward the mission of God, and the wife is called to the role of "yielding in love" to his leadership in God's divine mission. The mission of a surrendered life to Christ is the theme of Ephesians chapters 5 and 6—and the flow of the argument moves from men submitting to Christ, wives submitting to their husbands, and children submitting to their parents. It goes like this: Men and women submitting to one another "out of reverence for Christ" (5:21); wives submitting to their husbands "as to the Lord" (5:22); husbands loving their wives "as Christ loved the church," (5:25-30); the appeal to Genesis 2:24 (5:31); and the concluding summary (5:33)[42]; children obeying their parents "in the Lord," (6:1); and slaves are to obey their masters "as you would Christ." (6:5)

A wife cannot be in "sub-mission" to her husband if she doesn't know what the *primary* mission is! The greater challenge of Ephesians 5:21-24 is as much to the man as the woman. God's divine role is for the man to have a God-impassioned, Jesus-led, Spirit-empowered mission in leading his wife, and for the wife to follow her man into the mission. It's extremely difficult for anyone to submit to anyone or anything if the mission is not clear. Husbands, you absolutely need God's mission for your marriage! Wives, you are called by God to yield in love to the mission God is giving both of you.

A couple of years ago, during a very trying time in our ministry at Mountain Springs Church, I went through a period of deep depression, anxiety, and questioning of my calling as a pastor. The church had outgrown my abilities as a leader and administrator. I was constantly overwhelmed and felt as though I was cracking under the pressure. At first, Liz was very encouraging and accommodating in my struggle. But weeks lengthened into months, and my inner turmoil continued, until one day she pulled me aside and gave me one of those "Coach Liz in the locker room" talks. She basically said, "Look honey, I love you, and I really trust you. Don't hear me saying anything different. But, you have got to pull it together and seek God for your mission! The constant gyrations and questions must stop. If you are supposed to continue as a pastor here in Colorado, I'm with you. If God is moving us to something else, I'm with you too, but please seek the Lord and settle this now!" What a wake-up call. What a woman!

Following Liz's advice, I headed to a mountain cabin and sought the Lord in fasting and prayer for three days. God spoke to me during that time and settled my calling and mission. But if God had not used Liz to challenge me as the loving leader of our marriage and our home, I could easily have derailed everything.

Men, you must have a mission. Women, God has called you to yield in love to your man and the mission God has given. Thus, I believe that submission means:

- *Both husband and wife yielding in love to Jesus*
- *Both husband and wife loving each other with the power of the Holy Spirit*
- *The husband and wife seeking God for the mission of the marriage*
- *God speaking to the man for the family's mission and getting feedback from his wife*
- *The man leading and the woman encouraging and supporting the mission God has given*
- *The wife yielding in love to the leadership of her husband as he yields to the mission God has given*

Men, do you know where you're going with your life? Do you have a God-given mission for your wife and family? Your wife cannot follow a man who doesn't know where he's going! Someone has said that anyone who thinks he's a leader but finds no one is following is only taking a walk. Are you taking a walk or leading your wife?

THE POWER OF COMPLEMENTARY MARRIAGE

When I first met Liz, we were traveling through China with a Christian group, smuggling Bibles to the underground church. We were in a strange land with lots of time to talk. What intrigued me about Liz was just how weird she was. She never answered questions the way I would. When we talked about a subject, her perspective was vastly different than my own. I just couldn't figure her out! It bugged me but also captured my interest. When I asked her about her favorite music, she didn't even mention The Doobie Brothers, Lynyrd Skynyrd, or the Allman Brothers. (How pathetic!)

What is it about our psyche that God has created within us a desire for someone who is different from ourselves? Some have said that "opposites attract," and it does seem that this has been embedded into the universe. Even in the animal kingdom, we see the roles of male and female as different and complementary.

My family breeds Labrador retrievers. In the breeding process we observe the importance of the male (stud) dog's aggression and the female (dam) dog's role of submission for breeding to be successful. But it is even more than that. Once, while we were breeding one of our female Labs with a chosen stud, a stray dog—attracted by the smell of our "in heat" dam—wandered onto our property. You would have thought a gang rumble for dogs had occurred as the stud fought off the stray. It was cool to watch this dog protect and fight for his "damsel in distress."

God has given us the complementary relationship to strengthen the individual parts of a marriage. The traits that most often attract us to the opposite sex are usually our opposites. Like the north and south ends of a magnet, we are drawn to the differences of the other person. Yet often our biggest struggles later in marriage are the result of forgetting this. What we now think we "hate" are the very characteristics that first attracted us to the other. But, if we can grow to understand that God has given us a complementary marriage of leadership and submission, we can see the wisdom of God's divine roles in Ephesians. It is just what Solomon also points out:

Two are better than one,
Because they have a good reward for their labor.

For if they fall, one will lift up his companion.
But woe to him who is alone when he falls,
For he has no one to help him up.
Again, if two lie down together, they will keep warm;
But how can one be warm alone?
Though one may be overpowered by another,
two can withstand him.
And a threefold cord is not quickly broken.
Ecclesiastes 4:9-12

Liz, in her role as my complement, yielding in love to Jesus and me, empowers me to lead and love as Jesus. As John Piper writes, "Submission is the divine calling of a wife to honor and affirm her husband's leadership and help carry it through according to her gifts."[43] Her guidance to me, her gifts, her differences and fresh perspective, make me a stronger person, a better husband, a more loving father, and a more consistent leader. I'm a better man because of my wife. I'm a more sensitive leader because of her humble heart. I pray Liz is a stronger person because of my guidance in her life. She is a more joyful, fulfilled wife and mother because of my love for her.

Many women don't know how to yield in love, to biblically submit to their husbands. Because they never observed a truly yielded, loving marriage relationship between their mothers and fathers, this command seems too high a hill to climb. Most of us need some simple steps to follow to learn a new skill, but the good news, ladies, is that there are some simple steps you can follow to become more submissive, which will be a blessing to your husband. Here are a few simple steps.

A TRIO OF SIMPLE STEPS TOWARD A YIELDED LOVE

1. *Understand his talents and skills.* Encourage your husband in his God-given talents and skills.
2. *Discover together the mission.* Encourage, discuss, and pray with your husband and work together in discovering God's mission for your marriage.
3. *Study your husband.* Learn what he loves and needs from you ,and give yourself fully to meeting his needs.

Over the years, I have had the privilege of watching countless couples grasp the biblical teamwork of a complementary marriage—the husband lovingly leading with a mission, and the wife yielding in love and respect to her husband's leadership. The results are fascinating—husbands who begin fulfilling their calling to guide, protect, and passionately love their wives, and wives who enjoy the supportive role that encourage and build up their husband. Like a Broadway play, when each person understands the roles, a beautiful story can unfold.

Now listen up, men. The next chapter is by far the most important chapter of this book. To fully discern and understand your wife's needs, you must read this chapter. Your spiritual life and the future of your marriage depend on it. Chapter 4 could radically transform your whole life! I mean it.

So buckle up, grab a hot drink, settle into your favorite chair, start reading, and don't leave until you've read the entire chapter in one sitting. By the way, don't let your wife read this chapter before you do, or you will be in big trouble!

Conversation Starters

To the wife: Are you yielding in love to your husband? Why or why not?

To the husband: Are you lovingly leading your wife with a mission that you both have agreed upon? Why or why not?

What is God's purpose/mission for your marriage?

How can you each grow in your unique God-given role in your marriage?

CHAPTER 4:
ENTER AND DIE

We can never love somebody "too much." Our problem is that typically we love God too little. The answer is not to dim our love for any human in particular; it's to expand our heart's response to our Divine Joy.

Gary Thomas

Love must be learned, and learned again and again; there is no end to it. Hate needs no instruction but waits only to be provoked.

Katherine Anne Porter

Husbands, love your wives, just as Christ also loved the church and gave Himself for her.

Ephesians 5:25-26

When my father-in-law, Dick Perkins, was fresh out of college and a brand-new second lieutenant pilot in the Air Force, he had a harrowing experience on a routine instrument training flight on a North American T-6G "Texan." He tells the story of what happened:

Shortly after leveling off from a ninety-degree turn to the left to a heading of 180 degrees, it felt like I had over-controlled, the wings were banked to the right, and I should turn to the left to get the airplane level. I moved the stick to the left to level the wings.

"You're overshooting, Perkins," barked Mr. Reeves [the training instructor]. "Look at your compass."

He was right. The compass showed I was turning to the left and was now passing through 160 degrees, but the wings felt level. To move the stick back to the right would place us in a turn to the right. My mind was confused …

"You're still turning left, Perkins. Look at your compass and the artificial horizon."

I had definitely overshot the heading of 180 degrees and needed to turn back to the right. I moved the stick to the right to start turning back. When it felt like I was in a turn to the right, Mr. Reeves yelled at me again, "You got it level now. Let's turn to the right to get back to a heading of 180 degrees."

I thought, "Wow, he says we're level, and I'm definitely turning to the right. If I bank it any more to the right, we'll be in a steep turn and maybe end up in a downward spiral."

"Come on, Perkins, get the plane back to 180 degrees. Turn to the right."

He was getting impatient with me. I hesitated again because we seemed to be definitely in a fairly aggressive bank to the right already.

"Look at your instruments, Perkins. Tell me what they are telling you." I stared at the artificial horizon, and it showed the wings were level. The heading on the directional gyro (DG) showed 140 degrees.

"Well, sir, the DG shows we are on a heading of 140 degrees, and the artificial horizon shows a wings-level attitude."

"OK, so what are you going to do to get back to a heading of 180 degrees?"

I hesitated and then said, "I need to bank the airplane to the right. But we're already banking to the right. At least it seems to me like we are."

"No, we're not banking to the right. We are in a wings-level attitude just like you said we were. Look at the instruments. Do they tell you we're level?"

"Yes sir, they do, but we're definitely banking to the right."

"No, we're not. You've got vertigo. You have to believe the instruments no matter how it feels to you. Now fly the airplane by the instruments, not by the seat of your pants."

I moved the stick to the right and noted the artificial horizon began to show a twenty-degree bank to the right. The DG began to move and started toward the 180-degree mark. In my gut it felt like we were in a very steep turn, yet we were not.

"In instrument ground school they discussed vertigo with you, didn't they?"

"Yes sir."

"And didn't they tell you to not believe your senses but trust the instruments?"[44]

Aside from the name being used for the 1958 Alfred Hitchcock horror film, "vertigo" is a condition that can be very dangerous, especially when flying thousands of feet in the air. Vertigo is defined as "spatial disorientation;"[45] a sensation of spatial confusion. It's an inner-ear problem effecting equilibrium—being unable to discern balance and change. The term "vertigo" is often used when training pilots to fly airplanes.

Visual references provide our most important sensory information. In times of obscured or deprived vision (due to darkness, fog, or clouds) a pilot must learn to pay attention to his instruments or he will quickly become disoriented, which can lead to the "grave-yard spiral" and crash. This theory explains what happened to John F. Kennedy, Jr. on July 16, 1999, when the Piper Saratoga he was piloting crashed into the Atlantic Ocean off the coast of Massachu-setts, killing everyone aboard. The National Transportation Safety Board released an official statement that the crash was caused by "the pilot's failure to maintain control of his airplane during a descent over water at night, which was the result of spatial disorientation."[47] Kennedy was not instrument trained.

When being trained for night flying, for flying through storms and clouds where visibility is impossible, pilots are trained with a canopy over the windows of their plane. Visual aid is completely shrouded, and the pilot must learn to fly completely from the instrument panel, learning to trust it and not his feelings. The instrument panel gives the pilot information about the plane's speed, level, altitude, fuel, and all the other essential facts needed for a safe flight. The instru-ment panel is not hampered by the pilot's feelings. It never lies, and always leads the pilot in the right direction with perfect balance.

SPIRITUAL VERTIGO

If you truly long for a God-wild, adventurous, fulfilling marriage that will last a lifetime, you have to trust the instrument panel—God's Word, the Bible, God's Divine Order—not your past experience, your feelings, or how much darkness and fog is in your relationship right now. Or, as my father-in-law might say, *don't* "fly by the seat of your pants" in your marriage. Without a new focus upon God's promises and the power of His Word, spiritual vertigo will be the result.

Don't miss Paul's progression in Ephesians 5: He has told us that we must live in the power of the Holy Spirit (v. 18), and this leads to a heart and home full of praise and prayer (vs. 19-20), leading to a yielded love from the wife for her husband (vs. 21-24). Now he speaks specifically to the role of the man: *Husbands, love your wives, just as Christ also loved the church and gave Himself for her.* (v. 25)

Learning to love our wives "as Christ loved the church" is vertigo for men — the testosterone-laced, relationally challenged gender! If you're not already experiencing it, the feelings of spiritual and emotional dizziness begin now — with this chapter. Loving our wives like Christ is definitely "spatial disorientation."

If we trust our feelings, we are headed for a marital crash. Our natural instincts, our normal way of relating to our wives, has been embedded through our cultural cues of how to love. We have been steeped in the sexual revolution for the past forty years. We have all graduated from the "School of Cool" about masculinity and manhood. We cannot naturally and emotionally follow this command to radically love our wives. Our feelings are already screaming to our mind, "No way! I can't love like that every day! Impossible!"

ENTER HER WORLD

Our Instrument Panel says, "love your wives, just as Christ also loved the church and gave Himself for her." That means loving like Jesus loves. To love as Jesus loved, we must understand what Jesus did in loving us. Jesus willingly *entered our world and gave His life for us!* He willingly left the comfort and intimacy He had with His Father and entered our sin-soaked, rebellious, demon-saturated culture to sacrifice His life for you and me. He allowed himself to be broken, despised, whipped, and crucified for us.

Jesus loves His bride. In loving His bride, the Church, Jesus entered her domain and became sin at the cross. Jesus entered His bride's world — her humanity, her selfishness — and became like her — fully human. He took upon Himself our rebellion and died upon a rugged, cruel Roman cross. Jesus came with an unreserved, selfless, sacrificial love. He died for his bride!

Husbands, this is the kind of love we are being commanded to follow. We are being commanded to enter our wives' world and sacrifice our lives for them. We are being called to enter that estrogen-soaked place and die there! Just as Jesus willingly left the comforts and harmony of His world and entered our world and died, we also are to willingly leave the comforts of our safe world and enter into our wives' dangerous world. It's time to leave our natural feelings behind and trust our Instrument Panel!

Why? Because we are engaged in a risky and dangerous war. I hesitate to use the word "war," but indeed it is. Satanic forces are warring for your soul and the soul of your marriage. To enter into our wives' world and love them there brings out fear in all of us men. Many of us of the male gender have never experienced deep emotional intimacy (I'm not referring to the sex act)—and the mere thought of it is as frightening as a horror film.

At a recent conference, a young man waited until everyone had left the room before sharing his story with me, tears streaming down his face. He had grown up with a father who continually berated him as "gay" and "homo" because of his love for music and poetry. As a result, this young man had made an inner vow to cut off that part of his life and instead went to the extreme to compensate for what he was told was "real manhood." He shut down his heart. He shut down intimacy with himself and others. His marriage was in a "death spiral" because he could not open up and communicate love and intimacy to his wife.

John Eldredge has called this "the father wound." He writes,

> *"Every boy in his journey to become a man takes an arrow in the center of his heart, in the place of his strength. Because the wound is rarely discussed and even more rarely healed, every man carries a wound. And the wound is nearly always given by his father."* [48]

Every young boy grows up asking the question, "Do I have what it takes? Am I powerful? Until a man knows he's a man he will forever be trying to prove he is one."[49] Often, this unanswered question leads to defining intimacy through sexual exploits and extreme measures of violence or isolation.

For many men, the struggle for love leads to a pseudo-intimacy with women through pornography. Men are visually wired, and images and pictures arouse us much more than they do women. Eldredge explains the power of porn by writing, "That seductive beauty reaches down inside and touches [our] desperate hunger for validation as a man [we] didn't even know [we] had, touches it like nothing else most men have ever experienced."[50] Recent statistics would indicate that most men, even those in the church, are fighting a losing battle with pornography addiction.[51] This false intimacy erodes the true intimacy of loving our wives as Christ is calling us to do.

As a pastor of a church in a county where the divorce rate exceeds 60 percent, I see a marital landscape strewn with shattered husbands (and wives) who have mortal wounds of the soul that have brought death and carnage to themselves and their children. These men come to our church with no heart left for the battle. Like a Battle of Gettysburg for the soul, a "Civil War" where demons attack a man's heart, seeking to destroy all life and vitality. It is a fight for life and death. So it was at Little Round Top on July 2, 1863.

A closer look at that fateful day in Gettysburg reveals truth that also applies to our marriages. Colonel Joshua Chamberlain was stationed as the "anchor man" of the Union Army's left flank at Gettysburg. General James Longstreet of the Confederate Army, realizing that the weakest and most vulnerable line in the Union forces was at this point, concentrated his forces there. Wave after wave of volunteers from Texas and Alabama stormed the hill against Chamberlain and his 358 riflemen. Captain Howard Prince of the 20th Maine describes the fight that day:

Again and again, was this mad rush repeated each time to be beaten off by the ever-thinning line that desperately clung to its ledge of rocks. The two lines met and broke and mingled in the shock. The crash of musketry gave way to cuts and thrusts, grapplings, and wrestlings. The edge of conflict swayed to and fro, with whirlpools and eddies. At times I saw more of the enemy than my own men ... Five times [the Confederate Army] rallied and charged us.[52]

Realizing that he might not survive another attack, Chamberlain rallied every cook, wounded, sick, bandsman, and pioneer to his decimated line. Even two mutineers, who were prisoners, were given rifles with which to fight. Blood dripped from Chamberlain's foot, and he had a bruise on his left leg from a mine ball. And as the Alabamians and Texans prepared to attack again, it did not seem possible to Chamberlain that he could withstand another shock. That's when he heard the most frightening cry from his men: "Ammunition." The 20th Maine was out of ammunition![53]

In what is considered one of the most daring moves in military history, Chamberlain ordered his men to strap bayonets onto their empty rifles, rallied them to a suicide charge, and took the fight to the enemy. With Chamberlain himself leading the way, his men rushed down the hill into the teeth of the Confederate forces—and "the Confederates recoiled, so bewildered they did not know whether to fight or surrender."[54] Chamberlain and his men, far outnumbered, outmaneuvered, and totally out of ammunition, took more than 400 prisoners—and Little Round Top was secured. Some have said this single victory probably decided the war.

This is parabolic for our marriages. Men, we must take the fight to the enemy. It will take everything within us. It is a battle that is worth fighting for a bride worth loving. Our fight is for a deeper love relationship with our wives. Bruce Cockburn, the Canadian rocker, once sang, "Nothing worth having comes without some kind of fight."[55] And it is a fight indeed. It is a battle for our hearts; a battle for her heart. Our identity as men may not have come from our earthly fathers, but it can be reinstated by Jesus. Jesus entered our world and died for our hearts so that we might enter our wives' world and die for theirs!

FINDING INTIMACY

Even Jesus needed to find His identity for intimacy. Jesus found his identity in His Father's love. At His baptism, Jesus experienced the affirmation for intimacy as He was blessed by His Father.

> *When He had been baptized, Jesus came up immediately from the water; and behold, the heavens were opened to Him, and He saw the Spirit of God descending like a dove and alighting upon Him. And suddenly a voice came from heaven, saying, "This is My beloved Son, in whom I am well pleased."* (Matthew 3:16-17)

Jesus knew that He was pleasing to His Father for *who He was* and *whose He was.* Jesus understood and experienced the blessing of His Father. Jesus received affirmation from His heavenly Father which gave him a deep sense of security. It was from this affirmation of love that Jesus poured out his love for us. It was this promise of life for which Jesus could die to give us new life.

Like the first man, Adam, Jesus walked with His Father in constant communion. Robert McGee, in describing the relationship between Adam and God, could just as easily have been speaking of Jesus when he wrote, "the first created man lived in unclouded, intimate fellowship with God. He was secure and free."[56] This intimacy was rooted in knowing where and from Whom his significance came.

Men, do you know who you are? Whose you are? The power to enter our wives' world and die for them is a supernatural power rooted in our relationship of intimacy and identity with Jesus. Intimacy with our wives will be limited by our intimacy with God. As men, we must grow deeper in love with Christ, even as we die daily for our wives. Jesus once said, "Whoever seeks to save his life will lose it, and whoever loses his life will preserve it." (Luke 17:33) It is the marriage paradox: Dying to ourselves even as we live for Jesus; dying for our wives even as we live for our marriage. It was Dietrich Bonhoeffer who, paying the ultimate price on a Nazi gallows, said of following Jesus, "God calls us to come and die."[57]

But this death leads to a life of abiding—abiding in Christ. Jesus says to us, "Just as the Father has loved you, I have also loved you, abide in my love." Abiding in the love of God is the only means for loving our wives. It is the only true home for our hearts. We love out of an abiding intimacy with Jesus in our hearts. George MacDonald writes of this phenomenon:

> *When our hearts turn to him, that is opening the door to him ... then he comes in, not by our thought only, not in our idea only, but he comes himself, and of his own will. Thus the Lord, the Spirit, becomes the soul of our souls ... Then indeed we are, then indeed we have life; the life of Jesus ...*[58]

By surrendering of our lives to the power of Jesus, the Holy Spirit, we have the capacity to love our wives with the love of Jesus. We can enter their lives and die because we have entered into a life with Jesus and died. This death is an abiding life. It is what St. John the Cross called the "living flame of God."[59]

As we grow in knowing and loving Jesus we are given a new heart for our wives. When we enter her world, God wants to give us a new, reborn heart. This is the heart of Jesus being resurrected within us.

William Wordsworth captured the spirit of the new man, the new heart we must have with the words:

> *My heart leaps up when I behold*
> *A rainbow in the sky:*
> *So was it when my life began;*
> *So it is now I am a man;*
> *Or let me die!*
> *The Child is Father of the Man;*
> *And I could wish my days to be*
> *Bound each to each by natural piety.*[60]

Jesus' holiness, presence, and person are loosed within us. The child-like love we were all born with is longing to come out and live again, revealing the truly manly heart, and only possible through a growing death to self in order to live for Christ. Such a reborn life results in a sacrificial, giving, loving death for our wives.

DEFINITION AND DEMONSTRATION

More than just a definition for how a husband is to love his wife, we also need to see a demonstration of how it should look in the home. Marriage is action. We can read all the books, listen to all the tapes, go to all the seminars, and still skirt the issue. We are talking about a demonstrative action that can be seen and felt in the marriage. Our wives need tender treatment. It's almost like they have stamped on their foreheads the words, "Very Important—Handle with Care."

Entering our wife's world is as foreign for us men as entering another culture. Having traveled to more than thirty nations of the world and lived in several, I can tell you from experience, it's easier to get acclimated to a foreign nation's culture than to understand my wife's world! I think we should put a new ritual into every wedding ceremony—signing a passport before signing the marriage certificate. Learning her language, her unspoken cues, and loving her the way she needs to be loved is not easy.

Men and women are totally different physically, emotionally, and mentally. Marriage expert Gary Smalley explains, "The differences are so extreme that without a *concentrated effort* to understand them, it is nearly impossible to have a happy marriage."[61] For example, did you know that virtually every cell in a man's chromosomal makeup is different from those in a woman's body?[62] Even the "seat" of emotions in a man's brain is wired differently than a woman's.[63] Men and women are hard-wired completely differently by God.

Do you know what the major stumbling block is for most husbands in developing a God-wild, fulfilling, lasting, adventurous relationship with their wives? We fail to learn to love her from *her* viewpoint. Instead, we need to learn how to enter her world through the door *she* wants us to use.

Without understanding our wife's viewpoint, many a man's brilliant ideas can backfire. Like the time I bought my wife a specially made Indian sari while on an Asian tour. What was special to me wasn't very special to her. After opening the gift, Liz looked at me and said, "Interesting. Now when and where am I going to wear this?" It had never occurred to me that a brightly colored Indian sari just might not have a lot of uses in America.

Or the time I left Liz to go on a trip just one week after the birth of our son. This was when we lived in Okinawa—a foreign culture in which we had no family and few relationships. Liz had no help! Oh, and did I mention that she also had to take care of Anna, our firstborn, who was two years old? And oh, yeah, we had a home birth and no pediatrician! Yes, I was born yesterday! Guys, we have a lot to learn about meeting our wives' needs from their viewpoint.

To satisfy your wife, to enter her world, I believe you must make a dedicated, focused, concentrated effort to meet each of her needs. This stuff is not natural for us. Explained below are what I call "The Six L's to Loving Our Wives." I truly believe that as you master these six simple steps, you too can enter your wife's world and love her as Jesus loves you.

1. *Learn diligently.* Study your wife. Ask her what she needs and what kind of actions communicate love to her. Next to Jesus, your wife needs to know that she is the most valuable person in your life. She is more important than your job, your children, your hobby, and your friends.

2. *Listen deeply.* When your wife is struggling, stressed out, or just wants to talk, she needs to know that she can come to you and share her heart, and you will listen. Without giving explanations or trying to solve all the problems, we must learn to hear our wives' hearts.

3. *Lead gently.* She needs to know that you will guide, protect, and defend her with compassionate love. She needs to know that you're the kind of man that she wants her son to become and that her daughter would want to marry!

4. *Labor joyfully.* Your wife wants to share in every area of your life. Open up your life to her and let her in. She wants to feel like she is on your team, unified with joy.

5. *Love intimately.* Your wife needs to be held tenderly and often. Not only is the sexual relationship of intimacy very important, so are times of closeness and friendship outside of sex.

6. *Laugh frequently.* Your wife wants to have fun with you. Quit taking yourself so seriously—no one else does! Enjoy your wife—romance her, date her, laugh with her.

Entering our wives' world means that we will die! But death brings life. New life. When your wife's needs are met, she feels secure and glows with a sense of identity with you and Christ. Some of her glow will rub off on you. A happy wife is a happy husband, especially if you were a key part of giving her that happiness.

Conversation Starters

Husbands, ask your wife to share with you how you are doing in the six L's mentioned above.

Wives, explain to your husband how he can better "enter your world" and love you there.

Husbands, listen to your wife, write down what she says, pray over the list, and ask the Holy Spirit to empower you to change.

CHAPTER 5:
HAMMER, CHISEL, AND DEMONS

If marriage ... is a disillusioning experience for many people, the reason is to be found in the passivity of their faith. People dislike the fact that the blessings of God may only be found and enjoyed when they are persistently sought ... Marriage is, therefore, both a gift and a task to be accomplished.

Otto Piper

Wives, submit to your own husbands ... Husbands, love your wives as Christ loved the church ... that He might sanctify her ... so that He might present the church to Himself in splendor, without spot or wrinkle, or any such thing, that she might be holy and without blemish.

Ephesians 5:22-27

One of the most awe-inspiring natural monuments of God's creative power is the Rocky Mountains. Blessed to live in Colorado Springs, the front range of these handsome peaks is my daily view. During the winter, the snowcapped mountain of Pikes Peak is reminiscent of a dazzling ocean wave frozen at its crest.

Geologists theorize that the Rockies were formed through the shock and collision of the Pacific and the North American tectonic plates, causing a ripple effect that moved eastward, forcing massive amounts of rock to crack and slide over the terrain to form the mountains I now look at every day.

But without the massive collision of the Pacific and North

American plates, there would have been no shock wave—and thus no spectacular beauty to behold.

The marriage of two people, coming from different backgrounds, with vastly different personalities, of naturally antagonistic genders, is a recipe for a tectonic-like collision. But this shock can bring forth something very beautiful. Gary Thomas writes, "Beauty is often birthed in struggle. These points of impact may not be 'fun'—in fact, they can make us feel like we're being ripped apart—but the process can make us stronger, build our character, and deepen our faith."[64] Such is one of God's main purposes for marriage—transforming our character transformation and our lives.

"Collision" is inevitable in marriage. From house decorations to dinner menus, from work schedules to nasty habits, God has built natural shock waves into His design that demand from us a deeper understanding of suffering and conflict. Someone once said that if a marriage doesn't have conflict, either someone's not being honest or someone's not needed. Conflict in any relationship is inevitable and, if understood purposefully, can be one of the foundational factors for drawing us closer to Jesus and each other. Indeed, from God's vantage point, it seems that He has woven conflict into the marital cloth that makes up of the spiritual tapestry of maturity.

CROSSED COMMUNITY

The battle we face in marriage is not dissimilar to the life of Christ. In fact, we might argue that the reason God set up the relationship of husband and wife is for us to personally and daily experience the sufferings of Christ. Not a suffering for the sake of suffering, as some acetic, archaic, monastic, overly pious perspectives would have us believe, but rather the embracing of life—a life of communion with another person whom you choose to love—that leads to a purposeful, intentional suffering that if embraced, produces a fruitful joy and a robust maturity. The writer of Hebrews explains:

> *Therefore we also, since we are surrounded by so great a cloud*
> *of witnesses, let us lay aside every weight, and the sin which so*
> *easily ensnares us, and let us run with endurance the race that*
> *is set before us, looking unto Jesus, the author and finisher of*
> *our faith, who for the joy that was set before Him endured the*
> *cross, despising the shame, and has sat down at the right hand*
> *of the throne of God.* (Hebrews 12:1-2)

The Hebrews writer talks about the stuff of real living, real marriage—an earthy honesty—wherein we need Jesus and we emulate His journey, an adventure of endurance that could see through the agony of the cross to the joy on the other side. We must look through the translucent conflicts and suffering of our marriage and envision what's on the other side—the joy, the adventure, the power, and the God-wild transformation that is taking place in our lives as a result. Might it be that our spouse has crossed our life path to show us what the cross really means?

Marriage is a crossed community. We come to Christ through community (the church) and we grow into Christ through community. God invites us into the most formative of all communities through marriage. This most foundational form of community is the coming together of a man and woman in matrimony through Jesus Christ. "He is our peace" (Ephesians 2:14), and without His power for peace we live in a state of discord—between God and man and between man and woman. At the cross, Christ has become our mediator, our intercessor for peace. At the cross, His peace leads us into the power of the Holy Spirit, the power of praise and worship, and the power to deal with conflict through His manifest presence. Without Him we are doomed! Dietrich Bonhoeffer, in his great classic, *Life Together*, wrote:

> *Without Christ, we should not know God, we could not call*
> *upon Him. But without Christ we also would not know our*

brother, nor could we come to him. The way is blocked by our own ego. Christ opened up the way to God and to our brother. Now Christians can live with one another in peace; they can love and serve one another; they can become one. But they can continue to do so only by way of Jesus Christ. Only in Jesus Christ are we one, only through Him are we bound together.[65]

As we tap into the love of Christ that resides within us, we can deeply and affectionately love our spouses and enter true community. This love of Christ empowers our conflicts and resolves them. Yes, as crazily ironic as it might sound, love leads us into battle. It led Jesus into battle. Jesus went to the cross because of love. Jesus went to the cross for community with us. And so must we in marriage. The woman must go to the cross and enter a battle whenever she chooses submission to her husband. The man must die at the cross every time he chooses to enter his wife's world and love her like Jesus.

EMBRACING THE HAMMER AND CHISEL

Such conflict is purposeful so that through the collisions of marriage our character is etched out and carved into the character of Jesus. Paul is reminding us of the transformative purpose of marriage when he brings together the intentionality involved.

Wives, submit to your own husbands as to the Lord... Husbands, love your wives as Christ loved the church... that He might sanctify her... so that He might present the church to Himself in splendor, without spot or wrinkle, or any such thing, that she might be holy and without blemish. (Ephesians 5:22-27)

Like a divine sculptor, God is chiseling away our sinful nature through the hammer and chisel of that other person. Yes, He is using that other person to break our stony heart, to knife into our selfish edges, smoothing us into a new person with a new purpose and a new God-wild joy. This is the other side of the cross; this is the other side of marriage.

Yet, few marriages ever reach such a point of growth. Instead of embracing the hammer and chisel and allowing it to press us into Christ, we run! We run away from and over our spouses. We often end up fighting the wrong battles, the wrong way, turning them into the wrong war. Fought this way, the inevitable result is the destruction of the other person's self-esteem and character. It destroys community. Usually this leads to what has become the most popular of phrases, "irreconcilable differences" in marriage. Divorce is most often the result.

But God is not an uninvolved bystander. He has sovereignly given you that other person to chip and shave you into a new sculpture through the chisel and hammer of such conflicts. He is allowing struggles to enter our lives to change us. Job, whom God allowed to lose his fortune, family, and future to Satan's hand, said,

> *But now He has worn me out; You have made desolate all my company. You have shriveled me up … He tears me in His wrath, and hates me … My adversary sharpens His gaze on me. God has delivered me to the ungodly. I was at ease, but He has shattered me … He has set me up for His target … He breaks me with wound upon wound; He runs at me like a warrior.* (Job 16:7-14)

Ever feel that way about your marriage? We all have. It is obvious that Job understands God to be the ultimate source of his pain. Satan and his attacks are secondary—God is primary, and He is allowing and using such circumstances to transform us, to present us to Himself "that we might be holy and without blemish." Lon Solomon writes, "God orchestrates circumstances that touch every life to accomplish His perfect purposes. There are not accidents, coincidences, or acts of fate in this world."[66] This is the goal of marriage. This is the purpose of our life on earth.

DINING WITH DEMONS

Liz and I were calmly discussing a situation concerning our son's college hopes when she made a comment that just ticked me off. It was nothing—she just mentioned the need for us to trust God for the finances. But I wanted to kill her. I would have divorced her on the spot if I could have. I found myself uttering in my heart, "Does she think I'm *not* trusting God?" My spirit was blazing with anger. In just five minutes, our living room had become a war zone. You get the picture. You've all been there.

Where do such thoughts come from? All of those hateful thoughts and angry outbursts are not just from you. There is an enemy who is strategizing to ruin your life and marriage.

From the beginning, God has allowed Satan, once a guardian angel of the throne of God (Ezekiel 28:11-19 and Isaiah 14:12-14) and demons, fallen angels (Revelation 12:7-9), to buffer the marriage relationship. Satan and his hordes have been given permission by God to hold the hammer and chisel over our relationship with our spouse. It all started with the first marriage, just after the honeymoon, with Satan's stealth move upon Eve.

Therefore a man shall leave his father and mother and be joined to his wife, and they shall become one flesh.

And they were both naked, the man and his wife, and were not ashamed.

Now the serpent was more cunning than any beast of the field which the Lord God had made. And he said to the woman, "Has God indeed said, 'You shall not eat of every tree of the garden'?" And the woman said to the serpent, "We may eat the fruit of the trees of the garden; but of the fruit of the tree which is in the midst of the garden, God has said, 'You shall not eat it, nor shall you touch it, lest you die.' "

Then the serpent said to the woman, "You will not surely die. For God knows that in the day you eat of it your eyes will be opened, and you will be like God, knowing good and evil."

So when the woman saw that the tree was good for food, that it was pleasant to the eyes, and a tree desirable to make one wise, she took of its fruit and ate. She also gave to her husband with her, and he ate. (Genesis 2:24-3:6)

Satan, in his hatred of God and God's highest creation, has been maneuvering, navigating, and ambushing marriages from the start. In the millennia of his work, his strategies haven't changed. He is cunning and rarely reveals himself. He hides behind the ingenious disguises of personality, circumstances, weaknesses, pride, ambition, and power. Note the strategy with Eve: He moves in on a unified marriage, questions the love and goodness of God; he proceeds to twisting Scripture, then continues with the fascination of perpetual beauty and power.

Satan does the same thing today. The battle of the sexes usually revolves around the same issues: "You don't love me anymore;" "I can't believe you said that;" "We're just not on the same page;" "Who's in charge?;" "If I didn't have that woman strapping me down …" "If she would respect me, I would love her!;" Sound vaguely familiar? The strategy hasn't changed, only the words.

The Bible exhorts us to be aware or be in trouble, "lest Satan should take advantage of us; for we are not ignorant of his schemes." (2 Corinthians 2:11) The real problem lies in the fact that most of us *are* unaware of the schemes (the Greek meaning of the word is "strategies") of this enemy of God. We constantly find ourselves blaming our spouses and fighting with each other over his tactics.

Let's be clear about this warfare. Since Satan is a created being and neither omnipresent nor omnipotent, he can only be in one place at one time. Like any other created being, he (or it) is limited in scope and ability. Thus, more than likely, none of us will ever be tempted by Satan *himself*, but his demons take on his personality and tactics.

The names given in the Bible to Satan reveal much about how he navigates behind the scenes with his demonic "foot soldiers" to destroy our marriage relationships. In the Bible he is called: adversary, accuser, destroyer, murderer, lord of the house of bondage, worthless one, old serpent, liar, tempter, roaring lion, dragon, destroyer, devourer of men, and deceiver. Do any of those descriptions ever characterize your spouse? Your marriage? Yourself? Be honest.

Most often we unknowingly allow demons to enter our homes and eat at our tables through the fleshly sinful habits of our lives. Demons feed off the food we give them. The less our character is given to Christ, the more we give permission to the darkness. Demons cannot just enter our homes with no provocation. We open the doors and actually invite them to dinner by the choices we make.

Several years ago we bought an older home. When we moved in, we quickly realized that the place was filled with mice. From the crawl space to the attic, mice ruled this house. With a vision to remodel, we tore out the old fireplace, and from the hole in the floor where the fireplace had once existed came an army of little grey critters. It was gross. (As a result I have little fondness for Reepicheep, the cute mouse in the C.S. Lewis series, *The Chronicles of Narnia*.)

With some investigation, we came to understand that the mice were feeding off the water and food the previous occupants had left behind. With a systematic plan of tightening pipes, clearing out the pantry, and Terminex (!), we waged a winning battle against the nasty little Reepicheeps.

And so it is with demons. Like mice, demons need something to feed on if they are to enter and remain in our marriage. They feed off our sinful habits. As unfair as it may seem, demons are always on the lookout for people who are not surrendering certain areas of their character to Christ. They come in and invade our lives as we give them an open door through sinful weaknesses, unconfessed sin, unrepentant addictions, and bitterness in our heart. These open doors become footholds that turn into strongholds, which literally destroy our homes. The Bible teaches us that:

> *the weapons of our warfare are not carnal but mighty in God for pulling down strongholds, casting down arguments and every high thing that exalts itself against the knowledge of God, bringing every thought into captivity to the obedience of Christ.* (2 Corinthians 10:4-5)

Once I was called into a situation where a young captain in the Navy had tried to commit suicide. With a lustful desire for fame, he pursued his passion to be a world-renowned photographer, ultimately driving him into the arms of demons. Once, while taking black and whites at a Buddhist temple, he heard a voice in his spirit instructing him and guiding him. As the days stretched into months, this lone voice intensified, leading him into fleshly choices that ended up in drug addiction, infidelity, and divorce. He then tried to kill himself, just a month before calling me. But on the night I met him and in the months that followed, we cast out demon after demon, and saw a new freedom and joy come into his life. He gave his life completely to Jesus, began to renew his mind through the power of the Holy Spirit, and eventually got remarried to a wonderful young woman.

Paul understands the power of demonic footholds in our lives. He writes, "Be angry, and do not sin: do not let the sun go down on your wrath, nor give place to the devil." (Ephesians 4:26-27) The word "place" can be translated "foothold," and it has the meaning of a stirrup on a saddle, used for mounting a mule. The *Bible Exposition Commentary* says of this passage: "Satan hates God and God's people, and when he finds a believer with the sparks of anger in his heart, he fans those sparks, adds fuel to the fire, and does a great deal of damage to God's people and God's church. Both lying and anger 'give place to the devil.'"[67]

Anger in our hearts, or any other fleshly weaknesses, have the potential to become a stirrup that demons can use to mount us, in order to infiltrate and influence our lives and marriages. These fleshly areas of our lives, what the Bible calls the "old man" or old nature, (Romans 5-7) are the food of demons if we don't confess and confront them. Mark Bubeck explains,

> *The flesh is a deadly enemy which is capable of completely defeating a believer and keeping him from pleasing God with a holy life. One of the reasons the flesh is such a difficult enemy to handle is because of its close inner relationship to the believer's personality. The flesh is intimately intertwined with our mind, our will, and our emotions.*[68]

Importantly, we must identify and openly confront those sinful habits in our life that are warring against God and our marriage. The ways in which the flesh tempts us are found in such a list in Galatians 5:19-21. Successful victory over demons in our marriage demands that we become familiar with this list and seek God for His power to overcome.

In counseling embattled couples over the years, I would rank the following as the demonic footholds I most often observe:

- *Unwillingness to surrender over to Jesus issues of lust, anger, and unforgiveness*
- *Unwillingness to calmly and honestly communicate disagreements and hurt*
- *Living with secrets that cause bitterness, guilt, and division*
- *Undealt-with anger that spills out with each conflict*
- *Blaming others; an unwillingness to take personal responsibility*
- *Lack of unity on the use of finances*
- *Misunderstandings in how to communicate love and respect to the other person*
- *Lack of sensitivity to the spouse's sexual needs*
- *Unwillingness to forgive the spouse for something that happened in the past*
- *Inability to recognize personal needs and communicate them clearly*

If we are not vigilant in the fight, snares are awaiting us. In writing to Timothy, Paul said,

> *Flee also youthful lusts; but pursue righteousness, faith, love, peace with those who call on the Lord out of a pure heart. But avoid foolish and ignorant disputes, knowing that they generate strife ... be gentle to all, able to teach, patient, in humility correcting those who are in opposition, if God perhaps will grant them repentance, so that they may know the truth, and that they may come to their senses and escape the snare of the devil, having been taken captive by him to do his will.* (2 Timothy 2:22-26)

Without the power of the Holy Spirit in our marriages, without Jesus filling us with His love, compassion, and forgiveness, without praise and prayer with our spouse, we will not have the power necessary to "escape the snare of the devil." We will be captured by the powers of darkness and continually fight a losing battle against the enemy. The battle is fierce; understanding that it can be won is essential.

A FIGHT WORTH FIGHTING

John Eldredge has written, "A man needs a battle to fight, he needs a place for the warrior in him to come alive and be honed, trained, seasoned."[69] We as men were created to fight battles. We are the ones who enlist during wartime; we are the ones who get kicked out of school for fighting—usually over a girl. (In seventh grade, I once was jumped by a boy after school for writing a note to a particular girl!) God placed within all of us a passion for a warrior spirit that transcends our own desires for safety, something that longs to be on the front line of fighting for truth. We are called by God to be *His* ally in the fight of our lives—the battle for truth in our homes.

We got married because we believed that our lives would be richer, fuller, and more joyful because of our spouses. We have entered an arena full of conflict, and now the battle is being waged in our bedrooms, kitchens, and living rooms. Darkness wants your spouse as much as you do! Demons have entered your home, and they own your property unless you fight back. The time to fight is now! Not tomorrow, not next year, not when you feel like it, but right this moment.

A few months ago, I was meeting with a couple when the woman broke down in tears as she shared the loneliness she felt—the absence of connection with her husband—as he worked his way to ever-higher positions of power in the political realm. Both were successful in their careers, and both were longing for deeper intimacy physically, emotionally, and spiritually. But no one was willing to fight! No one was willing to battle for the other. I finally cried out, "Who in this office is going to war for this marriage? Who has the guts and courage to stand up and say 'enough is enough!' Who will fight for truth and kick the butt of Satan?" (I know what you're thinking. "Did he really say that?" Yes, I did. And I meant it.)

A fight is worth fighting for a love that is worth experiencing. Your marriage is the battleground that impacts your life and character more than any other. If you win in the home, you find the deepest, most God-wild, joyful, adventurous life possible. If you lose in the home, you lose almost everything. But God has given you a fight worth winning—because He's honing a character worth possessing. It is the battle itself that change us.

Gary Thomas says it well: "Jesus promised us that everyone will be seasoned with fire, and every sacrifice will be seasoned with salt (see Mark 9:49). The desire for ease, comfort, and stress-free living is an indirect desire to remain an 'unseasoned,' immature Christian."[70] The fight makes us stronger and deepens our faith. David expresses this bold passion with the words, "Blessed be the Lord my Rock, Who trains my hands for war, And my fingers for battle." (Psalms 144:1) And that is exactly what the battle is about—training us to face problems head on.

If your marriage is tough, get down on your knees and thank God for your spouse. Thank Him that He is training you for battle. He is forging character in you by your submission to Jesus and His sovereign plan for your life. You have a great opportunity, given by a God Who wants to use the fight to hone the warrior, to make your character more like His warrior Son, Jesus.

Jesus gave you that other person so that you would learn to fight for a God-wild, grace-filled, forgiving, adventurous marriage. In the meantime, He's transforming you into a more mature, loving, submitted Christ-follower. Your character is being forged into His—for His glory, His love, all the things we are called to live for anyway.

Jesus is our audience. We live for Him. Our marriage is about becoming like Him—growing to be more like Jesus in our attitudes and actions. Thus, the most difficult of marriages has the potential to produce the most meaningful of lives if we can see the opportunity disguised as a challenge. Look through a new lens at your marriage: How is he/she enabling me to grow closer to Christ through our struggles? How am I being changed by my marriage? What is it about my character that is being transformed through the battles of my marriage? Never lose hope. Hope sustains us.

> *Not only that, but we also who have the first fruits of the Spirit, even we ourselves groan within ourselves, eagerly waiting for the adoption, the redemption of our body. For we were saved in this hope, but hope that is seen is not hope; for why does one still hope for what he sees? But if we hope for what we do not see, we eagerly wait for it with perseverance.* (Romans 8:23-25)

When we place our hope upon Jesus, we can see a new man, a new woman, being formed through the conflicts of our lives. Be filled with the Holy Spirit; learn the habit of praise and prayer; willingly submit to him; passionately love her; and fight for your marriage! Like the stunning Rockies, God is pressing up a beautiful vista through the collisions of your marriage. He is using that other person to change and mold you.

Conversation Starters

What are the three most consistent difficulties of your marriage relationship?

How is God using these struggles to make you more like Christ?

Where have you allowed fleshly sinful habits to invite demonic strongholds in your personal life or marriage?

Will you willingly confess those areas to Jesus and repent today?

CHAPTER 6:
WILD SEX AND GLORY

Sexual intimacy and sexual climax get their final meaning
from what they point to. They point to the ecstasies that are
unattainable and inconceivable in this life.

John Piper

"[Sex] twice a week, hundred-four a year, should
give neither cause to fear."

Martin Luther

For this reason a man shall leave his father and mother and be
joined to his wife, and the two shall become one flesh.

Ephesians 5:31

layboy and *Penthouse* don't hold a fiery candle to God's design
for sex. If only people could *grasp* God's design for sex, men and
women would be turned on to a new, vital, dynamic, exciting,
rapturous perspective on the sexual relationship. God has designed
marriage to be a union of the spirits, emotions, minds, and bodies of a
man and woman who are wildly, passionately in love with Him and each
other. God designed the relational connection of a man and woman in
marriage to be a spiritual union, a mental union, an emotional union,
with the result being a wonderfully enjoyable physical union. This is
God's design for sex—passionate, intimate, and rapturous.

It should be no surprise to anyone who's been married very long to
realize that Paul only discusses the concept of physical oneness *after* he

has spent considerable time explaining how to get there. After sharing the necessity of being filled and empowered with the Holy Spirit, the power and necessity of praise and prayer, the role of the woman, the role of the man, and the importance of endurance, he now explains the result of such radical wild living: "For this reason a man shall leave his father and mother and be joined to his wife, and the two shall become one flesh." (Ephesians 5:31) The implications are obvious and clear—if you get aligned in the other areas, oneness follows.

Some have said that for women, sex begins in the kitchen. As a man, let me correct that: Sex begins as soon as you wake up. Or maybe before you get up if you have been hogging the bed all night.

Wild sex starts with a wild commitment to serving, submitting to and loving each other with the power and love of Jesus! Without the latter you will not experience the former.

God designed sex to be fun, adventurous, and deeply fulfilling through an ever-growing intimacy between a man, a woman, and God. Jesus wants your sex life to bring Him glory as you let Him guide your life. Sex brings glory to God when it is experienced through His design.

I can tell you from personal experience that the sexual relationship, done God's way, gets better and better as the years go by. As I've learned my wife's ways, as I've studied her, and as she has done the same of me, our physical union has improved. Do we still have our fights occasionally? Of course. Do we have many weeks when the job or the kids have worn us to a frazzle, and the thought of trying to turn each other on is a fading memory? Absolutely. Yet, our sex life has gotten better through experience, commitment, and years of hanging in there together. And so can yours!

SEXUAL CLIMAX AND THE KINGDOM OF HEAVEN

God has given no pleasure quite like the climax in the sexual union—almost an other-worldly experience. God meant it to be that way, an ecstasy like no other experience in this life. Through sexual climax, God is pointing us to a paradise to come. John Piper writes, "[Sex] points to ecstasies that are unattainable and inconceivable in this life. Just as the heavens are telling the glory of God's power and beauty, so sexual climax is telling the glory of immeasurable delights that we will have with Christ in the age to come."[71] The delight of reaching climax in the sexual union has been designed by God to give us a glimpse of the delight we will someday experience in heaven.

Sex within marriage is one of the most enjoyable and deeply fulfilling experiences of our marriage. To enjoy my wife's body in bed, to be caught up in the joy of experiencing the complete focus of my heart and body with hers, is unparalleled. Liz would agree. We have grown to understand each other through the sexual relationship. Sex has brought us together in deeper ways than we would have ever thought possible at the beginning of our marriage.

To have sex that brings glory to God touches our mind, our emotions, and our spirits at a level that points us toward the kingdom of heaven, what Gary Thomas describes as "sheer transcendence — brief, sunset-like glimpses of eternity."[72] God wants us to have such a sexual relationship. God even commands us to enjoy sex with our spouse. "Let your fountain be blessed, and rejoice with the wife of your youth. As a loving deer and a graceful doe, let her breasts satisfy you at all times; and always be enraptured with her love." (Proverbs 5:18-19)

Imagine that. God commands us to have fun, wild, enjoyable sex with our spouse! This is quite descriptive of just what we are "enraptured" by as men! Some translations say, "be intoxicated with her love." Others translate the verse as "ravished by her love." There is no feeling quite like the climax of sex. And God is commanding us to enjoy our wives' bodies. Such pleasure points us to the kingdom yet to come. Sex is a touch of glory!

Sex God's way culminates in climactic joy. Joy is supposed to be the result of sex. "Let your fountain be blessed, and rejoice with the wife of your youth." It seems pretty clear. Joy should be overflowing from a blessed fountain. Joy, as one of the fruits of the Spirit, is only possible through being filled and empowered by the Holy Spirit. Spirit-filled sexual intimacy brings joy and glory to God. This is God's design.

SEX DEFILED

Yet, most of us don't experience God's design. Instead, many of us are introduced to and grow up with sex as a shameful thing. Sex is a burden of guilt because of past sin and mistakes. Due to the wounds of pre-marital sex, pornography, incest, rape, or past hurt, the battle to see sex from God's perspective is perplexing at best and seemingly impossible at worst. One author captures this feeling with the words:

> *We are caught in the perplexity that sex often represents both the best and the worst moments of our lives. While sex may at times create moments that mark our deepest shame, it can also make us feel more free than ever before.*[73]

Sex is a channel of provision from God that nourishes part of our soul. Its pleasure feeds a deep emotional and physical need within us. However, with such pleasure, it can easily become an idol in our lives. Sex should nourish us, but we remember that never completely. The temptation to look beyond the Creator to the created is never greater than in the sexual realm. The writer of the Hebrews explains,

> *"Marriage is honorable among all, and the bed undefiled; but fornicators and adulterers God will judge. Let your conduct be without covetousness; be content with such things as you have. For He Himself has said, 'I will never leave you nor forsake you.'"* (Hebrews 13:4-5)

Consider how amazing it is that the writer places covetousness (most often exemplified through money) and sex side-by-side. The Second Commandment does the same: "You shall not covet your neighbor's house; you shall not covet your neighbor's wife ..." (Exodus 20:17)

The commandment is about an attitude — greed. Greed breeds behavior most often expressed through the lust for things — financial and sexual. Most marriage counselors today will tell you that the two major stumbling blocks to intimacy are finances and sex. The marriage bed and the use of finances are closely linked. Jesus said, "Where your treasure is, there will your heart be also." Money and sex are treasures that our head and heart are constantly drawn toward. Money and sex can easily draw us into lust and covetousness. Outside of God's design, they both easily can become idols. *USA Today* recently reported on a survey which revealed that most people think about finances between one and three hours a day![74] In 90 percent of divorce cases, arguments about money are prominent.[75]

The purpose of the passage in Hebrews is that "the bed be undefiled." Like money, sex can overwhelm our thoughts and lead us into covetousness and greed. In a private conversation, one noted counselor told me that "sex drives almost every area of a man's life." Such coveting of sex leads many into pornography, masturbation, and extramarital affairs. Satan knows the power of sex, and He has provided temptations that defile the person and derail the purposes of God. Sex outside of marriage defiles the delight of the kingdom of heaven in our hearts.

Sex involves three players — the husband, the wife, and God. God, who created the sex act, could have made it like changing your underwear each day. But He didn't. He made it potentially fun, exciting, even ecstatic. If we let God into our sexual relationship, if we will follow His design for marriage, we are letting the founder and inventor of sex into His adventure.

Godless sex is a travesty—to our hearts, our consciences, and our lives! Without God, the creator of sex, at the center of our sex life, the ultimate purpose and the ultimate pleasure of the process of sexual union is lost. Like the power of money and its potential to tempt us toward greed, dishonesty, and a lack of integrity, sex outside of marriage steals away the glory, joy, and ultimate purpose of God for our lives.

Solomon, in instructing his son, spends more than 30 percent of his biblical Proverbs talking about the power of sex. As the writer of the Song, Solomon was quite familiar with the highs and lows of the sexual relationship. In warning his children of the temptations of godless sex, Solomon writes of the crafty harlot,

> *Now therefore, listen to me, my children; pay attention to the words of my mouth: Do not let your heart turn aside to her ways, do not stray into her paths; for she has cast down many wounded, and all who were slain by her were strong men. Her house is the way to hell, descending to the chambers of death.* (Proverbs 7:24-27)

So we shouldn't be surprised that sex outside of marriage is so destructive. Tiger Woods' much-documented fall from grace is a modern-day, real-life metaphor for many today. Woods, arguably the greatest golfer of all time and definitely the highest paid, presented himself as the ultimate father and husband, married to a former model. He was blessed with talent, adoring fans, a beautiful wife, and two precious children. By all counts, he seemed to have it all. But, the lure of sex outside of God's design was too much. Even the world understands the difference between infidelity and integrity. As a result of the revelation of Woods' numerous affairs, he lost sponsorships from Gillette, Gatorade, AT&T, Accenture, and the playing editorship of *Golf Digest*, the world's largest golf magazine. Since the infamous car crash that led to the revelation of his many dalliances, Woods hasn't won a major golf tournament.

Many of us have a history of intimacy that isn't positive. Possibly through sexual addiction, especially through obsessing over the objectifying world of pornography, our physical relationships with our spouses have become disappointing and depressing. Some counselors speak of "Object Sex," or "Image Sex" to describe those who obsess over the images in pornography and then masturbate. This inevitably will deeply and negatively impact your sex life—and it's becoming a huge issue for both genders. Research has found a biological reinforcement that happens when endorphins are released in your brain as you connect with an image on a screen. You begin to have "object" or "image" sex, which actually begins to hinder your physical intimacy with your spouse.[76]

Image Sex addiction takes the beauty of a person and replaces it with an airbrushed, edited object that has no heart, no soul, and no spirit. In Image Sex our own hearts and spirits are compromised and stolen. Satan uses such false intimacy to destroy our spirits and frustrate our bodies. We become like the idols we worship—and make no mistake, Image Sex is idolatry. The Psalmist got it right when he wrote, "Their idols are ... the work of human hands. They have mouths but do not speak; eyes but do not see ... They have hands but do not feel; feet, but do not walk ... Those who make them become like them." (Psalm 115:4-8) We gradually become the sexless, spiritless, dead personification of the object we are staring at. The result is loneliness, deception, and a lack of unity with our spouse. Until one is willing to repent and turn away from such image idolatry, the joy of genuine intimacy will be missing.

Possibly due to attachment issues with one's father or mother—possibly deep incisions of the heart that have come through sexual trauma and broken trust—we have learned to guard our hearts like Roman garrisons. We have made vows that "no one is going to break my heart again." With such inner heart vows, we have hindered intimacy and love from entering our most private lives. Such resolve can kill your sex life! Such resolve can kill your spiritual life too. Doug Weiss, Ph.D., president of the American Association for Sex Addiction Therapy and clinical director of Heart to Heart Counseling Center, would call this "intimacy anorexia."

INTIMACY ANOREXIA

For many couples, the withholding of sex is a major problem. Weiss defines intimacy anorexia as "actively withholding intimacy from your spouse." The key word is "active." Often people say that they don't mean to withhold sex, but just like alcohol or drug addiction, this often goes on for years and it *has* become active and intentional. Not letting the other person into our spiritual and emotional life—not connecting even during the sexual act—is an addiction. Weiss identifies ten characteristics[77] of an intimacy anorexic:

1. Busyness. *Staying so busy you have no time for your spouse.*
2. Blame. *We want to be seen as good; thus, any negative input about your relationship results in blaming the other for the problem.*
3. Love. *Even when you know how the spouse wants to be loved, you actively withhold love.*
4. Praise. *Withholding praise from your spouse.*
5. Sex. *Withholding sex from your spouse; criticizing the other person about his or her sexual performance; not wanting to have sex.*
6. Spirituality. *Withholding spiritual connection from your spouse.*
7. Feelings. *Being unable and unwilling to share feelings with your spouse.*

8. Criticism. *Poking at the other in order to keep him or her distant in the relationship.*

9. Anger/Silence. *Shaming the other person through anger or silence to control and keep him or her distant.*

10. Money. *Controlling the money in order to control the other person.*

Weiss explains, "If you have five or more of these characteristics, you're most likely intimacy anorexic. That's where the cancer is in your life. That's not who you have to be or who you need to be. You can get healed. But we need a paradigm of what that tumor looks like so we can begin the road to recovery."[78]

All addictions and struggles in our lives are made up of choices, and these choices can begin to change as we submit our weaknesses to Christ. If five or more of the above signs are true in your life, and they continue after reading this book, let me encourage you to get help through professional counseling and use the workbook that Weiss provides for intimacy anorexia.[79]

Due to defiled sex and intimacy anorexia, Liz and I have been forced to watch helplessly as many marriages have met their demise over the years. From extramarital affairs and Internet porn to plain old boring, frustrated relationships, the aftermath has usually been distrust and the destruction of the marriage. Satan obviously understands the power of sex. Satan knows where our sinful triggers lie in manipulating and destroying our lives. Thus, it's no wonder that God has designed sex to actually be a weapon *against* Satan. Sex is one of God's most powerful warfare strategies for the destruction of Satan's work in our lives.

We have observed how many unhealthy women and men use sex as a weapon against their spouses. Women tend to do this more than men, but men are on the increase in using sex—either demanding too much or resisting any—to demoralize and frustrate the other.

My advice to men: Be romantic, loving, and sensitive before and during the sexual encounter; and to women: Proactively go after and encourage your man to have sex.

LOTS OF SEX AS A WEAPON AGAINST SATAN

God wants you to enjoy intimacy with your spouse and have lots of sex! It is no mistake that Ephesians 5 concludes with "the two shall become one flesh," and just twelve verses later says, "Finally, be strong in the Lord and in the power of His might. Put on the whole armor of God that you may be able to stand against the wiles of the devil." (Ephesians 6:10-11). Sexual intimacy with your spouse is spiritual warfare against the strategies of Satan.

Consider 1 Corinthians 7:5: "Do not deprive one another [of sex] except with consent for a time, that you may give yourselves to fasting and prayer; and come together again so that Satan does not tempt you because of your lack of self-control." God has ordained the sexual relationship to be a weapon against the temptations of the enemy. In the spiritual battle we are engaged in, frequent sex is important for victory over Satan and demons. John Piper writes, "For the people God leads into marriage, sexual relations are a God-ordained means of overcoming temptation to sin (the sin of adultery, the sin of sexual fantasizing, the sin of pornography)."[80] Lots of sex is important in fighting the temptations of Satan.

Liz and I have had many conversations about sex in our marriage. Through open and honest discussion about our differences, likes, and dislikes, we have learned to defer to the other frequently. Martin Luther, who understood the power of Satan, has been quoted as saying, "[Sex] twice a week, hundred-four a year, should give neither cause to fear."[81] Richard Baxter, the Puritan preacher said, "Keep up your conjugal love in a constant heat and vigor."[82] (And you thought Puritans never thought about such things?). Wow. The Bible even tells us that the man and woman do not have freedom over their own bodies. As married couples, we are given access and opportunity with our spouses' bodies:

> *Nevertheless, because of sexual immorality, let each man have his own wife, and let each woman have her own husband. Let the husband render to his wife the affection due her, and likewise also the wife to her husband. The wife does not have authority over her own body, but the husband does. And likewise the husband does not have authority over his own body, but the wife does.* (1 Corinthians 7:2-4)

My body doesn't belong exclusively to me. Liz's body doesn't belong exclusively to her. Though two individuals, through marriage we are becoming one! We are each other's body. We are each other's mind. We are each other's spirit. We are becoming one. This is the point of Paul's words, "the two shall become one flesh." Only as we walk with Christ, in the power of the Spirit, under God's design, do we begin to experience the wild adventure of my life becoming my wife's life and her life becoming my life. This is great news and great sex. We are sharing in the glory of God through mutual ownership of the other.

THE SEXIEST SONG EVER WRITTEN

Over the years, Lady Gaga, Madonna, and Britney Spears have created quite a stir with their sexual lyrics and videos. But no song has ever topped the steamy, erotic, and passionate description of sex recorded in Solomon's Song in the Bible. Yes, it's in the Bible! The subtle and not-so-subtle poetry with which Solomon evokes intense sensual awareness, while avoiding crude titillation, is the chief mark of this passionate work. Solomon, the poet, uses creatively the sensuality of nature by indirection and analogy, and captures vividly the emotional and physical love of a husband and wife. Every married couple should take time to read the Song of Solomon together, while in their bedroom with some great wine.

The love lyrics of Solomon capture the heart of God and His design for the sexual relationship between a husband and wife. It's an invitation into the glory of sex that is passionate, sensual, and exciting. Eugene Peterson, in his comments on the Song, writes, "It is very explicit sexually. The Song, in other words, makes a connection between conjugal love and sex—a very important and very biblical connection to make." Peterson continues, "Despite our sordid failures in love, we see here what we are created for, what God intends for us in ecstasy and fulfillment that is celebrated in the lyricism of the Song."[83] The Song is a convincing witness to just how God views sex.

The lyrical nature of the song is written in stanzas of two lovers sharing their feelings for each other. Like amorous love which is satisfying to both the man and woman, the poem moves back and forth from the husband sharing his heart to the woman doing the same.

Solomon opens his song getting right to the point of his poem: She: "Let him kiss me with the kisses of his mouth! For your love is better than wine; your anointing oils are fragrant ... Draw me; let us run. The king has brought me into his chamber." (Song of Solomon 1:1-4) No difficulties understanding what Solomon's wife has in mind for him that night. In his response, the man notices what every man would notice—the enticing outward beauty of his wife. "Your cheeks are lovely with ornaments, your neck with strings of jewels." (1:10) And her response to him speaks of her sensual preparation, "My beloved is to me a sachet of myrrh that lies between my breasts." (1:13)

The foreplay and actual sexual act is even described in a beauty unsurpassed in lyricism. "With great delight I sat in his shadow and his fruit was sweet to my taste ... for I am sick with love. His left hand is under my head, and his right hand embraces me! I adjure you, O daughters of Jerusalem, by the gazelles or the does of the field, that you not stir up or awaken love until it pleases." (2:3-7)

In describing his wife, Solomon seems to notice everything about her: "Behold, you are beautiful my love, behold, you are beautiful! Your eyes ... Your teeth ... Your lips ... Your cheeks ... Your neck ... Your two breasts ... You have captivated my heart, my sister, my bride ... A garden locked is my sister, my bride." (4:1-12) To which Solomon's wife replies, "Let my beloved come to his garden and eat its choicest fruits." (4:16)

The climax of the song culminates with these words:

Set me as a seal upon your heart,
As a seal upon your arm; For love is as strong as death,
Jealousy as cruel as the grave; Its flames are flames of fire,
A most vehement flame.

Many waters cannot quench love,
Nor can the floods drown it. If a man would give for love
All the wealth of his house, It would be utterly despised...
(Song of Solomon 8:6-7)

Solomon concludes his poem with three wise statements that characterize marital love as the strongest (*death*), most unyielding (*flames of fire*), and invincible force (*many waters*) in human existence. Just as death will not give up the dead, so love will not surrender the loved one. Just as flames of fire burn, so should our love continually be stoked. Just as floods of problems can overwhelm us, so should we be steadfast in our resolve.

God's strategy for the sexual relationship is beautiful and adventurous. If we will only take Him at His word and by faith trust our relationship to Him, He desperately longs for us to enjoy our spouses in emotional, mental, spiritual and physical intimacy. It is a fire that must be kindled. It is a passion that must be continually explored.

We should not be surprised. As John Piper writes, "Marriage at its exquisite peak of pleasure speaks powerfully the truth of covenant-keeping love between Christ and His church. And that love is the most powerful force in the world."[84] And so it is through the pleasure of climax in sex that we experience the pleasures of heaven. It is in the act of making love that we defeat Satan. And it is in discovering God's design for the marital bed that we come to most deeply grasp the unity of Christ in our marriage.

Conversation Starters

Ask each other what is needed to have a more fulfilling, rapturous sex life.

Ask each other what it is you enjoy most about lovemaking.

Ask each other what one or two changes need to be made for your sex life to take off.

CHAPTER 7:
THE DANCE

While differences between the sexes were part of the
original design of the God of the universe, they weren't built
in to create friction. Instead they were intended to
complement one another.
H. Dale Burke

Without love, she reacts without respect. Without respect,
he reacts without love — ad nauseam.
Dr. Emerson Eggerichs

Nevertheless let each one of you in particular so love his own
wife as himself, and let the wife see that she
respects her husband.
Ephesians 5:33

O ur Holt family enjoys dancing. On many Friday nights, we play
music and our kids, along with their friends, swing, throw, and
spin each other across the living room floor. We laugh as some
of their new moves end in abject failure.

Charity, our precocious six-year-old, is a Michael Jackson fan. She
cried uncontrollably when she heard that he had died. One of her
favorite movies is *This is It*, a compilation of interviews, rehearsals,
and backstage footage of Michael Jackson preparing for his series
of sold-out shows in London. What is most fascinating about the
movie is the meticulous care given to every step by each background

dancer—choreography that required perfect synchronized steps to the beat of Jackson's thumping musical cadence. As a former gymnast, I was amazed at each dancer's flawless routines.

Every dance, whether ballroom, swing, line, hip-hop, waltz, or concert choreography, requires teamwork, synchronization, and knowledge of one's partner. With each step, one must lead while another follows. At the heart, dancing involves teamwork. Arm, body, and foot movements require skill developed with practice through understanding and anticipating the other. If you've watched the TV show *Dancing with the Stars*, you've seen the beauty and beastly of what I'm talking about. Some of the dances on this show are engaging, but often, miscues happen, and quite frankly, the dancers can sometimes look horrible together—which is why we watch the show.

Marriage too is a dance. When two people are in sync—understanding and anticipating the other with grace, love, and a common mission—the dance is delightful. But, more often than not, our marriages look more like me when I pick up my Lab's front paws and pull her around the dance floor—stumbling and staggering along.

THE LOVE-AND-RESPECT DANCE

Paul, anticipating how differently a husband and wife respond and react to one another, gave us a secret into the delicate dance of marriage. "Nevertheless let each one of you in particular so love his own wife as himself, and let the wife see that she respects her husband." (Ephesians 5:33) Paul is emphasizing one of the key differences between men and women: love and respect. Women need to feel loved by their husbands, and men need to feel respected by their wives. It's as simple and as complicated as that. With love from the man and respect from the woman, the dance can be splendid and beautiful. Without it, disaster.

My wife loves simple things done with great love. Liz is neither extravagant nor expensive in her tastes—but she highly, and I do mean *highly*, values simple, caring, thoughtful acts that take *some* preparation and action. At Christmas, Liz and I often don't give each other the traditionally wrapped gifts placed under the tree, but rather several small gifts that are placed in the stocking over the fireplace. Several years ago, Liz told me that she wanted a particular perfume as her gift from me. Simple, easy to shop for, and inexpensive—perfect? Only if you can remember the name of the perfume. In my absent-minded way, I forgot it. The day before Christmas (because I *always* plan ahead!), fearing that I would mess up by giving her the wrong one and too prideful to ask her the name, I decided to give her a candle, a back scratcher, and a subscription to her favorite magazine, *Victoria*.

She was furious! The candle didn't match the living room, dining room, or bedroom (slight mistake); and since when is a back scratcher something every woman longs for? No further explanation needed. And to be honest, I didn't actually buy the magazine—I found it in the den and thought that Anna, our oldest daughter, had bought it. Turned out that Liz had bought it for herself! I had exhibited no forethought, and Liz did not feel loved.

A few years ago we were hanging out with the Mountain Springs Church pastors and their wives for a dessert. I was talking with one of the wives when suddenly, a cherry pie smashed into my face. All chatter and conversation in the room stopped and everyone stared at me. The culprit was Liz, and the reasoning was nonexistent. Liz later told me that she just impulsively had an idea to smash a pie in my face because she thought it would be funny. It wasn't funny, and I felt disrespected and embarrassed.

Dr. Emerson Eggerichs, in his best-selling book *Love and Respect*, wrote, "When a husband feels disrespected, it is especially hard to love his wife. When a wife feels unloved, it is especially hard to respect her husband."[85] When he doesn't feel respected and she doesn't feel loved, the misunderstandings and fights are guaranteed to heat up.

Women need to learn to use the word "respect" in communicating with their husbands. In one national survey by Decision Analyst, four hundred men were asked to choose which of two negative experiences they'd prefer to have: being left alone and unloved in the world or feeling inadequate and disrespected by everyone. "Seventy-four percent of these men said that if forced to choose, they would prefer being alone and unloved in the world," Eggerichs writes.[86] Being disrespected is one of the most negative experiences that a man can have.

My experience in working with men would confirm this. Men need love, too, but the feeling of love comes through respect. Respect covers a multitude of sins done to a man. A man who feels respected and honored is a man who has a much greater chance of reaching his full potential. Consequently, he has a greater capacity for love.

You see this with sports teams. When a coach shows his players respect and honor, you will see a team that wants to improve, wants to get better, and will fulfill its potential. Even when a player shows respect for his coach, it makes a difference. Coach Mike Krzyzewski, the legendary basketball coach at Duke, put this value into practice when he worked with the 1992 Olympians—the "dream team" on which Michael Jordan played:

> *After a team practice, I stood by myself on the sidelines drinking a Diet Coke. Michael Jordan walked over to me and asked, "Coach K, I would like to do about a half hour of individual work, and I was wondering if you could please work with me. So there I was, faced with a very difficult decision: working with the greatest basketball player of all time or continuing to drink my Diet Coke. I think I made the right decision.*

> *After our workout, Michael shook my hand and said, "Thanks, Coach."*

Michael Jordan had just called me "Coach," and he had said "please" and "thank you." This was at a time when he was at the very top of his game and was one of the most recognizable faces not only in sport but throughout the world. Michael Jordan had earned global recognition as a symbol of excellence. That day, I learned that everyone on Michael Jordan's team is treated with respect."[87]

The many military officers in our church have told me the entire armed service system is built on respect. If the men don't respect their superiors, at any level, trust is broken, the system breaks down, and lives can be put in jeopardy. For men to be willing to risk their lives for each other and die in combat, they must respect their commanding officer.

Men who feel respected by their wives are men who have the greatest possibility of growing in their love for them. I have yet to find a man who, when respected by his wife, doesn't want to provide and protect—and even to die if necessary. Men who are respected by their wives are men who will work hard to love their wives as Christ loved the church. Women, a word of advice: *Respect your husband. Try to see past his weaknesses to the heart of his need for your respect.* The result will be amazing.

I have heard many sermons on "unconditional love," but have yet to hear anything on "unconditional respect." But if, arguably, the man is to enter his wife's world and show unconditional love for His wife, just as Christ so loved us (Chapter 4), is it not true that a woman should show unconditional respect to her husband? I think so. If love is best communicated to men through respect, it absolutely must be unconditional. If love is what every woman needs, it must be unconditional. If not, with each changing circumstance, argument, struggle, and difficulty, we can toss our love and respect out the marital window.

A FAITH DANCE

We must learn the steps to a dance of faith. Unconditional love and respect is by faith, not by feeling. Feelings will flee and can't be trusted, but faith remains strong if we will call upon Christ for his power (Chapters 1-2). Women, you must cry out to God for the strength to respect your husband when he is not being very loving. Men, you must cry out to God for power to love your wife when she is not being very respectful.

Husbands—you have a faith job before you. To show love even when being disrespected is one of the most difficult faith challenges for a man. Men tend to lose their perspective and the heart they must have for their wives in the face of contempt. Though I'm speaking of unconditional respect, men must love back the respect they have lost. You win back respect by loving her with the faith that is beyond feelings. It is a faith love that breaks through her lack of respect.

I am currently working with a pastor and his wife who are on the verge of divorce. The wife has lost all respect for her husband, and she is ready to walk. The husband is crushed. It may take him years to regain this trust relationship, but what she needs right now is a man who will focus on her and love her unconditionally—even when he doesn't feel respected. And what he needs is a woman who will begin to grow and show respect, albeit by faith—not a feeling, even when she doesn't feel loved. If both will dance the dance of faith, we might see a homecoming.

COMPLEMENTARY STRENGTHS

One of the great lessons of the love-and-respect-dance is that each has a key part in the movement of the other. Our modern culture has devalued our differences in order to over-emphasize our sameness. The tendency today is to stress equality at the expense of minimizing our differences as men and women. John Piper explains,

This depreciation of male and female personhood is a great loss. It is taking a tremendous toll on generations of young men and women who do not know what it means to be a man or a woman. Confusion over the meaning of sexual personhood is epidemic ... The consequence is more divorce, more homosexuality, more sexual abuse, more promiscuity, more social awkwardness, and more emotional distress and suicide that comes with the loss of God-given identity.[88]

It is no wonder that our children today are confused about what it means to be a woman or man. Our media and culture has increasingly placed a premium on creating an androgynous view of gender. The result is a lack of clarity about our distinctive differences and complementary strengths. Yet, only in developing an appreciation of our spouse's strengths, and the teamwork and synergy it provides, do our homes find the strength needed to withstand the struggles we will face.

The faith dance of love and respect involves two people who utilize the individual strengths of each and thus enjoy the complementary unity of both. When a married couple can understand each other's differences and value the complementation they bring, beauty can be the result.

Such synchronized fluidity of movement captures our eyes and our hearts. This is most visible in figure skating. Every four years, our family gathers around the TV to watch our favorite Olympic competition (outside of gymnastics of course) — the pairs figure skating.

We will never forget the almost magical gold medal performance of China's Shen Xue and her skating partner Zhao Hongbo in the 2010 Winter Games. As soon as Shen and Zhao began, they had the crowd energized. The crowd cheered wildly for every element they landed. When they finished their routine, Zhao knelt on the ice and buried his face in his hands. Shen gently placed her hand upon his back. Zhao and Shen are not only world pairs skating champions, they are also married.

They skated with the passion that has become their trademark, their choreography perfectly in tune with their music, "Adagio in G Minor." Shen was so expressive, the audience could feel her every emotion. And despite being veritable senior citizens—she was 31 at the time and he was 36—they showed the world the beauty of complementary unity. Their throw jumps were huge and flawless, the kind of tricks that would dazzle even the X-Games generation. Each jump, each throw, and each spin depended on the other person doing his or her part with excellence. Without Zhao's strength, Shen would never have the height for her axles and toe loops. Without Shen's beauty in the air, Zhao would be just another skater.

And marriage is the same. We each have our parts to play and our strengths to bring. The sad part is that many of our marriages more closely resemble MMA cage fighting than pairs figure skating. Instead of complementation, we see competition. Instead of drawing from the other's strengths, we can tend to tear down the other's weaknesses.

Yet God has given us a partner with strengths we don't possess. Without him, you are incomplete; without her, there is a hole in your life. You need each other.

Growing up, I knew my mother to be a strong woman—a Southern steel magnolia who could manage her two boys with vigor. My father often left early for work and came home late. Much of my time before and after school was spent with my mom. I learned that my mother was omni-competent. She could manage the home, finances, yard, and me with half her brain tied behind her back. She was also an excellent leader and teacher. She was often in demand as a speaker at parenting and communication seminars. Her leadership qualities were quite strong. My fourth-grade teacher once complained to my mother that "Steve talks too much in class! I see more of the back of his head than the front of his face." Her response shocked my teacher. "I know. But you need to remember that his father is a preacher, and I talk more than his father, so the poor kid can't get a word in edgewise at home. So the only place he can talk is in your class." Needless to say, my mom didn't win any points with that teacher, but she sure did with me.

They were a terrific team. My dad, who planted and pastored six successful churches, was the unchallenged leader of our home. My dad has told me on several occasions that he could never have led so many successful churches without mom's strength and support. My mom, who was often called upon to pack up and move with my dad (they moved eight times), was fond of saying that her many ministry opportunities only increased with each new location. Even with such gifting, I never felt any competition between them. Dad lovingly led my mom, and Mom respectfully followed Dad.

THE FRIENDSHIP FACTOR

The basis for the love-and-respect dance is a friendship with your partner. Without friendship, a couple cannot even step on the dance floor. Liz and I once met a woman who was a card-carrying, self-proclaimed expert in the area of friendship. I'm not kidding. We met this lady at a bed and breakfast in Oxford, England, twenty-four years ago, and we've never forgotten her. When she introduced herself to us (and all the other guests at the inn), she handed out her business card to everyone, and it read "Ph.D., Friendship."

The only problem was that she was one of the rudest, most self-centered, most easily offended people we had ever met. At breakfast, she cussed out a German fellow who didn't agree with something she said. She dominated every conversation, and we couldn't get away from her fast enough. She quickly became known throughout the house for doing the oddest things. During one of the few nights we stayed there, I got up to use the community bathroom. When I opened the unlocked door, I was shocked to find her lying in the tub, facing me, in all her glory, this friendship expert! When she saw my surprise, she said calmly, "Hey, baby!" (If this woman had not been in her seventies and weighed about three hundred pounds, I might have negatively interpreted her greeting.)

Here was a woman who thought she understood—and even advertised herself as an expert in—the intricacies of friendship. She was fooling herself but no one else. Don't miss this point. So many of us walk around our homes thinking we're connecting with our spouse (and children), but we are not willing to examine our words, thought processes, and ways. We are systematically dismantling the friendship factor, all the while thinking everything is just fine.

The Bible says, "A man who has friends must himself be friendly. But there is a friend who sticks closer than a brother." (Proverbs 18:24) Friendship involves being friendly. What a novel thought. Liz has said, "In marriage, we think we have a right to be our worst with those with whom we are most familiar." Instead of building on and building into our spouses, we take them for granted, and the friendship factor is left untended.

Liz and I believe that a friendship with Jesus and each other is the foundation for a fulfilling long-term marriage. Friendship is the basis for love and respect. It is impossible for a man to genuinely love his wife without a growing, developing friendship. Similarly, it is impossible for a woman to respect her husband without feeling a sense of relational friendship.

Four friendship factors must be in place for love and respect to characterize a marriage. I believe that without these factors growing and developing in a relationship, the foundation for love and respect will eventually crumble under the pressures of life and conflict. The four Friendship Factors are:

1. **The Missional Factor.** Marriage is a partnership with a mission. I talked about the importance of this in

Chapter 3, with the word "sub-mission." Every couple needs to have a common mission for their friendship. What is the legacy of your marriage? Why has God put you together with your spouse? A couple with a common mission can withstand great issues and struggles.

2. **The Emotional Factor.** Learning to relate to each other on an emotional level is vital to a continuing friendship of love and respect (Chapter 4). That means helping, caring, giving, talking, praying together, and complimenting each other. Work hard to find the emotional side of your life—this makes the friendship a deeply growing adventure of the heart.

3. **The Forgiveness Factor.** Friends hurt each other. The closer you get, the more you notice the other's weaknesses and struggles. This inevitably leads to frustration, hurts, and misunderstandings. Couples who effectively weather storms and attacks on their unity are people who have learned to be unoffendable and forgiving. The power of God is the only answer to animosity and bitterness. Forgiveness is the antidote.

4. **The Fun Factor.** Friendship has to be fun. Yes, joy must be a key factor in any marriage. If you're not having regular fun, then take a day off from work and spend the first half doing something fun that your spouse enjoys. Then take the second half doing something you like! Have fun! Enjoy your relationship and enjoy sharing your hearts together. This should be the result of a God-wild, adventurous life together.

THE UNOFFENDABLE MARRIAGE

The offendable spirit is deadly to friendship. The easily offended person never grows in love or respect. People who are easily offended stumble through relationships that become close and then are torn apart; tight, then loose; close, then distant. Sad is the offendable spirit of a man or woman who can't seem to make the adjustment to the give and take of relationships. I liken it to the difference between a rose bush and a pine tree. A rose bush need lots of sunshine, almost perfect conditions of heat—consecutive warm days and nights to grow and survive. If the conditions aren't perfect, the rose bush just will not grow. The "rose bush person" is easily offended and unforgiving. If you don't say the right things, in the right way, at the right time, they carry a grudge—and your life becomes like a spy novel of trying to solve the mystery of what makes this person happy. What a drag!

In contrast, a pine tree easily grows and flourishes under almost any weather conditions. Even extremely cold weather and altitude don't negatively affect a pine tree. A "pine tree person" is not easily offended, and is able to find his way through the maze of complicated relationships. They are people who tend to think the best of others and give people the benefit of the doubt.

I want to be a pine tree in my friendship with Liz. I want to continually grow in allowing Liz to be imperfect and give her the freedom to make mistakes. Since I need the same grace because of my relational clumsiness, I must give it. I've made it one of my goals in life to try to live an unoffendable, pine-tree life. I cannot be a friend to Liz if I am easily offended.

Some of you are rose bushes—so easily offended that everyone in your life feels like they are walking on eggshells, trying not to upset your fragile little apple cart. You struggle to maintain friendships that are genuine and free because you are so easily hurt. If someone looks at you the wrong way, disagrees with you, or challenges your thinking, you blow up or distance yourself from the relationship. You will never have close friendships or reach your full potential in your marriage.

Let me challenge you. Love and respect are built on factors

found in friendship. And friendship is only maintained by living an unoffendable life. The unoffendable person is one who can look past the other person's moods, rudeness, and mistakes. The unoffendable person is basically a friend who can stick close through hard times, look at the deeper intentions of the heart, and not be so easily swayed by outward actions that aren't truly representative of the other person's motivations.

The unoffendable life means that you can overlook petty issues and believe God for a greater, more lasting objective. Living the unoffendable marriage enables you to have love and respect that can have time to grow and flourish under many varied and different circumstances. Unoffendable love is stable, strong, mature, and willing to forgive. Unoffendable respect is a deeply maturing understanding of the other person that believes the best, gives room for mistakes, and understands that there is a commitment to working things out. The unoffendable friendship is the balance to the hard days, when one of us loses control and the other needs to respond with love and respect, even when we don't feel like it.

THE UNORIGINAL ORIGINAL DANCE

And so we dance. Marriage is a dance that involves all the elements and steps found in this book. It is always original and yet unoriginal at the same time. Every marriage has its own set of issues and unique qualities that are shared only between you and your spouse. Your dance is unique and original, and God meant it to be that way.

But the God-wild marriage is unoriginal. I love it when people tell me that my teaching and thoughts are unoriginal. This book is an integration of Scripture (Ephesians 5:18-33) and my own experience in working with married couples. Thus, I have no interest in breaking new ground in teaching but rather stimulating interest in the new and untested ground of integrating ancient Scripture into modern-day marriages. So few counselors today, especially those that purport to be Christian, use the Bible as a basis for their advice that it has seemed right to challenge our marital worldview with God's perspective.

So, each concept found in this book is from God's Word. It is unoriginal in principle, yet original in practice. My prayer is that you and your spouse will apply each of these concepts to your own lives. I also pray that you will both find an original dance that allows you to experience a God-wild, adventurous, rapturous, fun marriage.

Why not do something original and unoriginal? Take God at His Word — unoriginal — and apply it to your marriage — original — and watch what He will do. Let go of the high bar, embrace that moment of fear and faith, and start living fully with a growing trust that the Holy Spirit can empower you into a God-wild love for your spouse that will change your life forever.

Turn on the music, grab your spouse by the hand, and dance the God-wild marriage!

FAQS

With twenty-six years of marriage and fifteen years working as a pastoral counselor of married couples, certain questions have become predictable. They seem to come up in every discussion, argument, and counseling session. Unfortunately, some of these questions were not covered in this book.

This last section is meant to give a few quick responses to questions couples most often ask about their marriage that I have not touched on yet. In light of the fact that I have attempted to be true to the text of Scripture in Ephesians 5, as well as the limited focus of my thesis, I fully realize that some questions will remain unanswered. This section is to provide the kind of answers and resources I often give married couples.

It is true that men and women approach life in general and marriage in particular from opposite ends of the spectrum. Men and woman view things differently, and thus ask very different questions. The gender differences drive our thinking. In light of this need, I'd like to respond to both male and female perspectives.

Times are changing. Life is speeding up. The doubling of knowledge has gone from being every seventeen years (after World War II) to every eighteen months. To add to our continuing knowledge base and growth with the twenty-first century couple, we conducted a survey in February 2011 with our 3,000-member congregation at Mountain Springs Church to discover where our married couples "itch" in their marriages, the questions they have, and the struggles they are encountering. This epilogue reflects the conclusions from our survey.

My prayer is that this will be a fitting and helpful conclusion as you move forward with passion into a God-filled, Spirit-empowered, Jesus-loving marriage.

1. How do we develop and/or maintain our romantic love? How do we keep the spark alive?

This is an important question. More and more couples are dealing with unfaithful spouses. The meteoric rise of extramarital affairs is alarming. Pornography on the Internet, men traveling more, and women working outside the home have all added to the "temptation factor" in our daily lives. When romantic love is lost, affairs can often be the result.

I believe the loss of romance is related to needs being unmet by one's spouse. Unmet needs within the marriage often lead to longings and hopes for needs to be met in other relationships. When needs go unmet, the romantic love, the feelings of passion, are lost in the marriage. This can lead to an emotional affair, a physical affair, or both. While working with couples, psychologist and marriage counselor Dr. Willard Harvey, Jr. made an interesting discovery in this regard:

> *I counseled the next couple to do whatever it took to make each other feel good and avoid doing what made the other feel bad. They were able to restore their romantic love and their marriage was saved. From that point on, I simply asked each spouse what the other could do that would make him or her the happiest ... my success rate skyrocketed ... Before long, I was helping almost every couple fall in love and thereby avoid divorce.*[89]

Later, Harvey identified the most common needs for men and women. He found that when the spouse met those needs, romantic love could be restored. When romantic love is restored, the chance for a happy, fulfilling, God-wild marriage increased exponentially.

Here are Harvey's discoveries, which also are the chapter titles in his book, *His Needs, Her Needs*. I would encourage couples to put their greatest effort in restoring a romantic love for each other into these actions, and also to read the entire book.

1. *The first thing she can't do without—affection*
2. *The first thing he can't do without—sexual affection*
3. *The second thing she can't do without—intimate conversation*
4. *The second thing he can't do without—recreational companionship*
5. *She needs to trust him totally—honesty and openness*
6. *He needs a good-looking wife—physical attractiveness*
7. *She needs enough money to live comfortably—financial support*
8. *He needs peace and quiet—domestic support*
9. *She needs him to be a good father—family commitment*
10. *He needs her to be proud of him—admiration*

Romantic love is a litmus test for how couples are caring for each other. Caring love demonstrates a passion for a God-wild, Spirit-empowered adventure with your spouse. One of the most important ways we can affair-proof a marriage is through caring and loving enough to meet the other person's needs.

2. How do I encourage my husband to be the spiritual leader of our home?

Men don't naturally lead spiritually in the home. They will lead at work, in recreation, and in a hobby, but most will not lead effectively in the home unless they are willing to grow. In my opinion the problem lies in a cultural misunderstanding among men concerning the workplace and the home. Men work hard at work and tend to view the home as a respite, a place to rest. In order to change their perspective, men must grow in a fresh understanding of their role as a spiritual leader. I believe it's possible for the home to be a place of rest *and* a place for leadership. The following are some practical steps that we believe will help develop a new mindset in your man:

A. *Provide a home of rest and relaxation, especially when he just gets in from work. If both of you work, then both will need to provide a place of rest for the other.*

B. *Encourage him in a loving, caring, and non-emotional way to lead the home spiritually. And whenever he makes an effort, applaud and thank him. Men need tons of encouragement.*

C. *Give ideas that are practical and easy. For example, if you eat supper together, show him devotional materials that are available and easy to use after a meal. Encourage prayer together just before bed, etc.*

D. *Attend a church where the pastor(s) encourages men to spiritually lead in their homes.*

E. *Attend a small group where there are strong men leading the group and their families.*

F. *Build friendships with couples led by strong spiritual husbands who will model the kind of lifestyle and leadership needed. Men need mentors and models in their life.*

G. *Be sure that he has read this book from cover to cover. (Best marriage book around! Right? Well, I might be exaggerating slightly.)*

The bottom line is that a man must want to grow spiritually before he can lead spiritually. If he has read this book, then he must want to grow. Talk about this issue. Share your heart and encourage him and love him through the process.

In my opinion, if a man would just do these three things in his marriage, it would radically transform his home:

A. *Lead your family to a Word-filled, Spirit-filled church, and attend weekly.*

B. *Initiate and lead a family prayer time daily or at least a few times each week.*

C. *Initiate and lead a Bible reading time, preferably the same time as prayer.*

3. What do I do about my in-laws? They are very intrusive in our marriage.

This hasn't always been easy for us. For the first few years of our marriage, I deferred to my mother on many questions, and this was frustrating for Liz. Once, while in a heated debate, I finally "got it" (look, I'm from Georgia and it takes me a while. I'm slow, but I get there eventually!) and understood Liz's frustration. Then I changed. I first needed to stand up to my mom. In a teary exchange, I talked with her about why she needed to honor Liz, as well as why it was necessary for me to lead Liz, even when that meant having a disagreement. Over the following years, my mother changed, I changed, my preferences and priorities changed—and God has given us victory since that time.

Remember the Bible is clear in saying, "a man shall *leave* (my italics) his father and mother and be joined to his wife, and they shall become one flesh." (Genesis 2:24; Matthew 19:5; Mark 10:7; Ephesians 5:31) Mentioned four times in the Bible, God wants us to understand what I call the "Leave and Cleave Principle." When you marry, you leave your old family of origin and cleave to your spouse, forming a relationship that will eventually lead to a new home and family. It's the only way forward.

If you don't truly leave, you can't genuinely cleave. The emotional ties to the original family must be redefined in order to embrace the new relationship. I'm not speaking of lessening one's honor or love for our father and mother, I'm speaking of a redirection and redefinition of love for our parents. I still deeply love my mother and father and always will. But my marriage to Liz changed the direction of my affections. My primary affections are now for Liz more than for my parents. Liz takes precedence. Liz's opinions and desires are a higher priority for me than my parents'. Liz and I confer and have conversations before I discuss issues with my parents. My wife trumps my mom, and I trump Liz's mother and father on issues related to our immediate family. If you want to cleave, then leave!

4. We just can't agree on finances. What do we do?

It is rare for a couple to naturally have harmony in finances. In most marriages, one spouse is a spender and the other is a saver. Usually one is more concerned and the other less involved. In most cases, one is more uptight and the other loose as it relates to money management. So, how in the world does a couple find any form of harmony or compromise in financial matters?

Over the years, Liz and I have had major differences over the use of money. She was raised in an upper-middle-class home, and I grew up in a pastor's home with money savers all around me. My parents were sticklers about saving, getting deals, and finding the sale of the century. I grew up on Goodwill and garage sales, and Liz shopped at Dillards and Macy's. Need I say more?

A woman should marry a man for his money! Every woman I've ever met wants her husband to make enough money to meet their basic needs. Women don't mind working, and many today do work, but the problem arises when they *have* to work to make ends meet. I think every man should provide enough money to meet the needs of a wife and family. The Bible tells us the same thing. Read 2 Thessalonians 3:10-12, Hebrews 13:12-10, and the books of Ecclesiastes and Proverbs. A man must financially provide for his family.

In the past fifty years we've seen a revolution in the workforce, and women have flooded the marketplace. Today, there are more women graduating from college than men. Women outnumber men in the job market also. So one would think that the view of men being the main providers should have changed, but apparently, women haven't gotten the memo. There is even evidence of growing resentment among women for having to work outside the home.

Men, let me share a few key thoughts on money management that might help:

- *Learn how to budget.* If you don't know how, find a good money manager, a book, or attend a Dave Ramsey seminar.
- *Most women don't mind working but get upset if they have to work.* So develop a Needs Budget that only includes the husband's salary. You can then develop a Wants Budget that includes both incomes.
- *Agree on **and stick to** your budget.* If you can't meet your budget each month, then you must downsize. Most couples would rather have less and be happy than have more and be miserable!
- *Talk about money with your spouse as often as necessary.* But don't scream and holler. Grab a warm cup of coffee and work through the budget dollar by dollar.
- *Learn the principle of 80-10-10.* Spend 80 percent, save 10 percent, and give 10 percent. I've always followed this guideline, even during the lean years of graduate school and when I was starting the church with nothing. It worked, and we have had financial harmony through the years.

5. We fight too much. How can we communicate better?

Liz and I communicate often. Sometimes our conversations turn into a war of words. One time, our discussion ended up in a sock fight. She was folding clothes when our slight disagreement turned into an octagon match, so she began throwing socks at me and I returned them. Fortunately, we soon realized the stupidity of our battle, and eventually broke down laughing.

Every healthy couple should fight from time to time. If you're having occasional fights, it means you're communicating. Two people from entirely different backgrounds should have differences of opinion. So a verbal disagreement, or even a healthy fight, is not all bad. In many cases, if you learn to fight the right way, it's healthy and *good*.

Tone matters. Before anyone can have better communication, the super-charged atmosphere of heated anger must dissipate. Communication works best under calm circumstances. This means sharing one's heart is important. The more a couple takes time to talk from the heart, the chance for full-on heated debates will lessen.

Here are some guidelines that will make your disagreement conversations (and there should be many of these), not disagreeable in tone, but disagreements in content.

- Make regular time for sharing your hearts with each other. *The more often you make time for healthy loving conversation, the less time will you have for over-the-top blow-ups.*
- Learn to listen before being listened to. *Ask your spouse questions and draw out her feelings, desires, hopes, and fears.*
- When you feel a disagreement starting to brew, talk about it. *Like boiling water, before the whistle blows, take the pot off the fire, and talk about the issue. "I can tell you're getting upset*

about ..." "Let's talk about how you feel ..." "Did I hurt you when I ...?"

- Practice "I" message listening. *Instead of using "you" statements to rip the other person apart ("You always ...!" "You never ...!"), try taking responsibility without attaching value to your statement. ("I feel hurt when you ..." or "I was disappointed when you ..." or "I don't think you meant this, but when you did ____, I felt angry. Can we talk about it?")*

- Go on Question Dates. *In order to strengthen your friendship, grow more deeply in love, and understand the other better, go on dates during which all you do is ask questions of the other. A few sample questions:*

  1. When you want to relax, what do you enjoy doing? Why?

  2. If you could have your perfect vacation, if money wasn't a problem, what would you want to do? Why?

  3. If you had a million dollars, what would you do with it? Why?

  4. If you could live anywhere in the world, where would you want to live? Why?

  5. What are your deepest dreams for your life?

  6. What is your perfect job? Why?

Now you try it. Make up your own questions. I hope this can help get you started on the most fulfilling relationship of your life—falling in love again and again with your spouse. So jump in today and refresh, rejuvenate, and resurrect your love for each other. A God-wild marriage is as close as your spouse.

Carpe Diem Gloriae Dei,
Steve

ENDNOTES

[1] Paul Tournier, *A Place for You*, (New York: Harper and Row, 1968), 163.

[2] Cornela King, *First Comes Love, Then Comes Mortgage*, Internet article and survey. http://zine375.eserver.org/issue1/living4.html.

[3] *The Dictionary of the New Testament, Part I*, (Grand Rapids: Zondervan, 1986), 654.

[4] from "Marriage" in the *International Standard Bible Encyclopedia*, revised edition, (Grand Rapids: William. B. Eerdmans Publishing Co., 1979), 375. The *International Standard Bible Encyclopedia* explains further, "In analyzing the institution of marriage in the Bible, one finds that figurative language is very important ...The unity, sacrificial love, and interdependence usually associated with marriage enable the individual to comprehend, in part, the unity, love, and interdependent features of God's relationship with His people under the symbols of God's covenant with Israel and the Church as bride and body of Christ."

[5] Dr. George W. Knight III article, "Husbands and Wives as Analogues of Christ and the Church," found in *Recovering Biblical Manhood and Womanhood*, (Wheaton, Ill.: Crossway Books, 1991), 165.

[6] R.Kent Hughes, *Ephesians-The Mystery of the Body of Christ*, (Wheaton, Ill.: Crossway Books, 1990), 15.

[7] John Piper, *This Momentary Marriage*, (Wheaton, Ill.: Crossway Books, 2009), 11.

[8] W.J. Larkin, Jr., *Culture and Biblical Hermeneutics*, (Grand Rapids, Mich.: Baker Book House, 1988), 109, noted by Dr. George W. Knight III article, ibid, 171.

[9] *The commands of Ephesians 5 are often not our natural responses or feelings. They don't fit most postmodern psychological paradigms or popular cultural teachings on marriage. Thus, the principles of Ephesians on marriage are not the typical teaching in most marriage books and conferences.*

[10] Many studies confirm this: For example, the "Historical Shifts and Beliefs have Weakened Marriage," by Glenn Stanton, July 8, 2009; The Muhlenberg College study, "Do Break Ups Cause Break Ins," by Kate Bartkus, Kristin Cahayla and Christi Ulrich

[11] Pew Survey, *Time Magazine*, Dec 4, 2010, 50.

[12] Ibid.

[13] Ibid.

[14] Dr. John Gray, *Men are from Mars, Women are from Venus,* (New York, New York: HarperCollins Publishers,1994).

[15] T.S. Eliot, "East Coker," in *The Complete Poems and Plays, 1909-1950,* (New York: Harcourt, Brace, and Co., 1952), 129.

[16] Eugene Peterson, *Christ Plays in Ten Thousand Places,* (Grand Rapids: William B. Eerdmans Publishing Co., 2005), 1.

[17] W.H. Gardner and N.H. Mackenzie, ed., *The Poems of Gerard Manley Hopkins,* (London: Oxford University Press, 1967), 90.

[18] William Law, *The Power of the Spirit,* (Ft. Washington, Penn.: Christian Literature Crusade, 1971), 18.

[19] Eugene Peterson, *The Message,* John 15:1-7, (Colorado Springs, Colo.: Navpress, 2002).

[20] Craig S. Keener, *IVP Bible Background Commentary: New Testament,* (Westmont, IL: InterVarsity Press, 1993).

21 John and Paula Sandford, *The Transformation of the Inner Man,* (Tulsa: Victory House, Inc., 1982), 245.

22 Gary Thomas, *Sacred Marriage,* (Grand Rapids: Zondervan, 2000), 22-23.

23 I am indebted to C.S. Lewis for his book *The Four Loves,* and Dietrich Bonhoeffer's book *Together* for this understanding.

24 Mort Fertel, *Marriage Fitness* website, marriagemax.com.

25 Frances de Sales, *Thy Will be Done: Letters to Persons in the World,* (Manchester, N.H.: Sophia Institute, 1995), 42.

26 "Voice Change," *Science and Nature: Human Body and Mind,* BBC website, November 7, 2009, http://www.bbc.co.uk/science/humanbody/ body/articles/lifecycle/teenagers/voice.shtml.

27 Gary Thomas, ibid, 237.

28 Ibid, 237.

29 Howard Markman, Scott Stanley, Susan Blumberg, Natalie Jenkins, and Carol Whiteley, *Twelve Hours to a Great Marriage,* (San Francisco: Jossey-Bass, 2004), 21.

30 Ibid.

31 I am indebted to Jack Taylor and his writings in *The Hallelujah Factor* for aspects of this insight. *The Hallelujah Factor,* (Bungay, Suffolk, UK: Highland Books, 1983), 21.

32 Ibid.

33 *Strong's Exhaustive Concordance,* Hebrew 34:27.

34 Jack Taylor, 25.

[35] Ibid, 33.

[36] *Twelve Hours to a Great Marriage*, 125.

[37] Dietrich Bonhoeffer, *Letters and Papers from Prison*, (London: SCM Press, 1953), 28.

[38] John Piper, *This Momentary Marriage*, (Wheaton, Ill.: Crossway Books, 2009), 99.

[39] *Strong's Exhaustive Concordance*, 5293.

[40] Wayne Grudem and John Piper, ed., *Recovering Biblical Manhood and Womanhood: A Response to Evangelical Feminism*, (Wheaton, Ill.: Crossway Books,1991), 168.

[41] John W. Ritenbaugh, from *Forerunner Commentary*, Bible Tools on the Internet, www.bibletools.org.

[42] Dr. George Knight III, ibid, 165.

[43] John Piper, ibid, 101.

[44] Dick Perkins, *Air Force Days—Book One*, (self published, 2006), 28.

[45] Ibid.

[46] Ibid.

[47] NTSB accident report NYC99MA178, Dec. 12, 2000.

[48] John Eldredge, *Wild at Heart*, (Nashville: Thomas Nelson Publishers, 2001), 60.

[49] Ibid, p. 62.

[50] Ibid, p. 91.

[51] Recent data from Barna Research would indicate that 65 percent of men have a porn addiction.

[52] Willard M. Wallace, *Soul of the Lion*, (Gettysburg, Penn.: Stan Clark Military Books,1960), 97-98.

[53] Ibid, p. 100.

[54] Ibid, p. 102.

[55] Bruce Cockburn, "Lovers in a Dangerous Time," *Stealing Fire*, 1984.

[56] Robert S. McGee, *The Search for Significance: Seeing Your True Worth Through God's Eyes,* (Nashville: W. Publishing Group, 1998, 2003), 13.

[57] Dietrich Bonhoeffer, *The Cost of Discipleship*, (New York: Touchstone Books, New York: 1959), 122.

[58] George MacDonald, *The Heart of George MacDonald*, quoted from *Wild at Heart*, 131.

[59] St. John of the Cross, *The Living Flame of God*.

[60] William Wordsworth, *The Major Works*, (London: Oxford Press, 1984), 246.

[61] Gary Smalley, *If Only He Knew*, (New York: HarperCollins Publishers, 1979), 7.

[62] Ibid.

[63] Ibid.

[64] Gary Thomas, *Sacred Marriage*, (Grand Rapids: Zondervan, 2000), 128.

[65] Dietrich Bonhoeffer, *Life Together*, (New York: Harper Collins,1954), 9-10.

STEVE HOLT

66 Lon Solomon, *Brokenness*, (Potomac, Md.: Red Door Press, 2005), 14.

67 *The Bible Exposition Commentary*. (Colorado Springs, Colo.: Chariot Victor Publishing, 1989)

68 Mark Bubeck, *The Adversary*, (Chicago: Moody Bible Institute, 1975), 28.

69 John Eldredge, *Wild at Heart*, 140.

70 Gary Thomas, *Sacred Marriage*, (Grand Rapids: Zondervan, 2000), 129.

71 John Piper, *This Momentary Marriage*, (Wheaton, Ill.: Crossway Books, 2010), 128.

72 Gary Thomas, *Sacred Marriage*, (Grand Rapids: Zondervan, 2000), 200.

73 Ibid.

74 *USA Today*, January 7, 2011, 2A.

75 Randy Alcorn, *The Treasure Principle*, (Sisters, Ore.: Multnomah Publishers, 2001), 52.

76 For more information on this issue, go to www.sexaddict.com.

77 Douglas Weiss, Ph.D., *Intimacy Anorexia*, (Colorado Springs, Colo.: Discovery Press, 2010).

78 Ibid.

79 Dr. Douglas Weiss provides a DVD and workbook for Intimacy Anorexia. For more information, call 719-278-3708 or email heart2heart@xc.org; www.intimacyanorexia.com.

80 John Piper, ibid, 133.

81 William H. Lazareth, *Luther on the Christian Home*, (Philadelphia: Muhlenberg Press, 1960), 226.

82 Quoted from *Sacred Marriage*, 204.

83 Eugene Peterson, *The Message: The Bible in Contemporary Language*, (Colorado Springs, Colo.: NavPress, 2002).

84 John Piper, ibid, 135.

85 Dr. Emerson Eggerichs, *Love and Respect*, (Brentwood, Tenn.: Integrity Publishers, 2004), 16.

86 Professional survey data quoted in *Love and Respect*, quoted from *For Women Only*, (Portland: Multnomah Press, 2007). Survey performed for Shaunti Feldhahn by Decision Analyst.

87 Mike Krzyzewski, *Beyond Basketball*, (New York: Warner Business Books, 2006), 140-1.

88 John Piper and Wayne Grudem ed., *Recovering Biblical Manhood & Womanhood*, (Wheaton, Ill.: Crossway Books, 1991), 33.

89 Willard F. Harley, Jr, *His Needs, Her Needs*, (Grand Rapids: Revell, Baker Publishing Group, 2011), 12.